UNASSAILABLE

UNASSAILABLE

Inside a Three-Billion-Dollar Arbitration and the Brief That Could Not Be Ignored

Andy M OJI

COSMOLAWS

Unassailable: Inside a Three-Billion-Dollar Arbitration and the Brief That Could Not Be Ignored

This is a true account based on the author's personal experience, recollections, and professional judgment. To protect parties and ongoing legal matters, names and certain identifying details have been changed or omitted. Where events are described, they reflect the author's perspective and understanding. Others involved may characterise these events differently. The essential facts as the author experienced them are accurate to the best of his knowledge and belief.

ISBN: 978-978-68-4570-8 (paperback)
ISBN: 978-978-68-4571-5 (hardback)

Published by:

COSMOLAWS
7 Jay Momoh Street
Ajao Estate
Lagos
Nigeria

First Edition

Also by Andy M. Oji

Negotiating Aircraft Operating Lease

International Aircraft Leasing and Financing

The Principles and Practice of Aircraft Wet Leasing

Unassailable

Dedication

To those who choose evidence over authority, principle over convenience, and integrity over institutional acceptance—even when the cost is high.

Epigraph

When dispute resolution loses its integrity, the cost is not borne only by the parties. It is borne by nations, economies, and the rule of law itself.

Contents

About the Author

Andy Oji is a legal practitioner and partner at COSMOLAWS, a specialist aviation and arbitration law practice based in Lagos, Nigeria. With over thirty-five years of experience in dispute resolution, he has acted as counsel and arbitrator in more than ninety ad hoc and institutional arbitrations conducted under the ICC, LCIA, AAA/ICDR, and UNCITRAL Rules, involving disputes across multiple jurisdictions and legal systems.

His practice spans complex, high-value matters in aviation, joint ventures, mergers and acquisitions, construction, energy, banking, and defence contracting. He is particularly experienced in managing disputes where technical complexity, sovereign interests, and strategic judgment intersect.

Before joining COSMOLAWS, Mr Oji served as General Counsel of Bellview Airlines and later as General Counsel and Chief Risk and Regulatory Compliance Officer at First Nation Airways. This dual perspective—as in-house counsel responsible for operational, regulatory, and risk management challenges, and as external counsel and arbitrator in international proceedings—has shaped his practical and principled approach to dispute resolution.

Mr Oji has authored three influential books on aviation law. *Unassailable* is his fourth book, recounting his experience as counsel in a five-year international arbitration involving a three-billion-dollar claim against the Government of Nigeria. It reflects on the ethical, institutional, and professional challenges that arise when legal process, power, and principle collide.

Author's Note

This book is a personal account of my experience as counsel in an international commercial arbitration involving a sovereign state. It is written as a work of documentation and reflection on what institutional safeguards mean in practice.

To protect ongoing legal processes, client confidentiality, and individual privacy, names and certain identifying details have been changed or omitted. No confidential legal advice or privileged communications are disclosed. The events described are drawn from my personal experience, contemporaneous records, hearing transcripts, and publicly available or formally tendered materials. Where opinions are expressed, they reflect my professional judgment formed in the course of these proceedings. Others involved may characterise these events differently, and I acknowledge that my account reflects my perspective as counsel for one party.

The purpose of this book is not to challenge arbitration as a concept, nor to suggest that bias or impropriety is inherent in arbitral proceedings or among decision-makers. Rather, it examines—through documented personal experience—the structural vulnerabilities of ad hoc arbitration when broad discretion operates without sufficient institutional safeguards, oversight, or accountability. It explores how power, pressure, professional hierarchies, and procedural control can influence process and perception, and how disciplined advocacy, careful evidentiary construction, and strategic restraint can nonetheless compel lawful outcomes.

Dispute resolution systems are not merely technical mechanisms; they are institutional infrastructure. Their credibility shapes public trust, investor confidence, and economic development. When such systems function well, they support stability and growth. When they fail—or are perceived to fail—the consequences extend far beyond the parties to any single dispute.

The arbitral tribunal rejected my challenge to their independence and impartiality. They denied the allegations and ruled that they could continue serving. Where I express conclusions about conduct, these reflect my professional beliefs and observations formed during the proceedings, not established legal findings. I cannot know others' subjective motivations; I can only describe the patterns I observed and documented. I have endeavoured throughout to distinguish clearly between fact, inference, and opinion.

Nothing in this book alleges or is intended to suggest criminal conduct—including bribery or corruption—or any other legal wrongdoing. Where I describe concerning patterns or raise questions about procedural decisions, I am addressing institutional and structural issues, not making allegations of wrongdoing.

This book is offered in that spirit: as a contribution to an ongoing conversation about justice, accountability, and the quiet courage sometimes required to defend them.

Throughout the chapters that follow, descriptions of procedural conduct, statements made during hearings, and institutional responses are presented as they appeared to me at the time, based on the record as it then existed. Where language reflects concern, criticism, or strong professional judgment, it should be read in that context: as contemporaneous assessment by counsel charged with protecting a client's rights, not as retrospective findings of fact or assertions of personal motive.

Acknowledgements

This book represents five years and eight thousand hours of work—not all of it mine.

To the three senior lawyers who fought beside me through every procedural battle, every late night, every moment when the tribunal's conduct tested our resolve: your skill, dedication, and unwavering integrity made victory possible. I do not name you here—not because your contributions deserve anonymity, but because the nature of this account might invite consequences neither of us chose. You know who you are. You deserved better than what followed.

To the support staff who managed the mountains of documents, the endless correspondence, and the relentless demands of a case that consumed our practice for five years: thank you for your patience and professionalism. I protect your privacy for the same reason.

To the Special Assistant at the Office of the National Security Adviser: when institutional memory had faded, critical documents had disappeared, and personnel who had been involved in the operation were unavailable to testify, you did everything humanly possible to make the defence viable. You reached out to other government departments—the Central Bank, Customs, security agencies, archives—searching for the crucial evidence we needed. You understood what was at stake when others preferred distance. Your tireless efforts, your courage, and your principled support made victory possible. The government was fortunate to have you. Without your efforts, three billion dollars would have been lost. The nation owes you a debt it will never know it owes.

To retired Colonel Bello Fadile: when I reached out to you for help in defending our country, you agreed without hesitation. While others distanced themselves from a sensitive and controversial matter, you stepped forward—not for personal gain, not for recognition, but because the nation needed someone who knew the truth and had the courage to speak it. You provided critical information that shaped our defence. You testified about the negotiation and execution of the settlement agreement—testimony that became foundational to our victory. Your credibility, your clarity, and your unwavering commitment to truth made the difference between a viable defence and an impossible one. You are a great patriot. But more than that: you represent the best of what public service should be—principled, courageous, and selfless. Thank you not only for your role in saving three billion dollars, but for a career spent in service to Nigeria. The nation is better because you served it.

To the military officer who testified for the government with courage and integrity: I cannot name you here, and you would not want me to because the nature of this account might invite scrutiny you do not deserve. You know what you did. Your testimony deconstructed claims that might have otherwise succeeded. Your calculations proved accurate—vindicated by the Award itself. More importantly, when faced with a choice between personal gain and duty to country, you chose honour without hesitation. You represent the best of military service. Thank you for your courage and your service. The nation you serve is safer because of people like you.

To my partners and colleagues at COSMOLAWS, who carried the firm's work while this single case demanded so much of my time and attention: thank you for your understanding and support.

To Pascal Heath, Eric Murphy, and James Pete Scott: You happened to be in my office on September 6, 2024, when the Award arrived. You witnessed the scream, the relief, the raw emotion of complete victory after five years. Pascal, when you looked at me moments later and said, "You should write a book about this," I wasn't sure. Eric and James, when you both agreed and encouraged me to pursue it, I began to consider it seriously. Thank you for recognising that the story mattered beyond just the outcome.

To those who will read this and face similar choices—whether to challenge impropriety when they see it, or to accept it quietly for the sake of an easier path: I hope this account proves useful. The cost is real. The consequences can be severe. But the choice matters anyway.

Some things are worth the price.

Prologue

Two Envelopes

By the time the arbitration ended, five years had passed, and three billion dollars had been saved.

The notification of the Award arrived during a meeting on foreign investment in Nigeria's commercial aviation sector.

I was seated across from three international investors, walking them through regulatory frameworks, market access issues, and risk considerations—leases, bilateral air service agreements, enforcement realities—when my phone lit up on the table between us.

I glanced at the screen more out of habit than interest.

The subject line made my heart stop: *in Arbitration - [REDACTED] v. Federal Government of Nigeria.*

I picked up the phone. My hands were steady—thirty-five years of legal practice had trained me to maintain composure—but something in my face must have changed because the lead investor paused mid-sentence.

"Mr Oji? Are you alright?"

I opened the email. Scanned the summary. The words blurred, then sharpened into focus with devastating clarity.

The Arbitral Tribunal has rendered its final Award. The Federal Government of Nigeria has prevailed. The Claimant's claim for approximately US$3,000,000,000 is hereby dismissed in its entirety.

I screamed.

I actually screamed—a sound I hadn't made since childhood, raw and unfiltered. The investors jumped. One knocked over his water glass. I was dimly aware of the cascade of liquid spreading across the polished conference table, soaking into someone's portfolio documents, but I couldn't stop staring at my phone.

I reread it. Then a third time.

Total victory.

Complete vindication.

Three billion dollars. Gone. Vanished. The bogus claim I'd been fighting for five years, the mountain of distorted and unsupported arguments, the tribunal that had announced during the hearing they already had "a full picture" and "a position," yet spent twenty-five months deliberating before ruling completely in our favour. All of it collapsed, resolved in our favour. The government had won. Not a partial victory. Everything. I had won.

I took a moment to compose myself, then returned to the conference room.

"Gentlemen, I apologise for the interruption." I sat down, placed my phone face down on the table, and smiled. "That was notification of an Award in a case I've been handling for the past five years—a three-billion-dollar arbitration for the Federal Government of Nigeria. We just won. Complete victory."

The room went silent.

"Three billion?" the lead investor finally said. "American dollars?"

"American dollars."

He let out a low whistle. "Well. Congratulations." He glanced at his colleagues, then back at me. "I think we can certainly understand if you need to reschedule this meeting."

"No need," I said, though my mind was already racing ahead, wanting to read the full Award, to check for conditions or qualifications, to forward it to my team. "We were nearly finished anyway. Let me conclude our discussion, and then I'll need to attend to this properly."

We spent another fifteen minutes wrapping up. I functioned on autopilot—answering questions, providing clarifications, and scheduling follow-ups. Professional to the end. But my thoughts were elsewhere.

Twenty-five months I'd waited for this. Twenty-five months of what felt like resistance before the inevitable. And they'd had no choice. The evidence was too strong. The arguments were unassailable.

As the investors gathered their materials to leave, the lead investor paused at the door.

He studied me for a long moment, then smiled. "That's the kind of lawyer I want on my side." He extended his hand. "Congratulations. That's remarkable."

"You know what you should do?" he said. "You should write a book about this. Three billion dollars? There's got to be a hell of a story there."

I smiled. "You have no idea."

"Then write it. The world needs to know how this kind of thing gets done. Especially in emerging markets." He extended his hand. "We certainly need to know."

I promised to consider it and apologised again. We shook hands, they left, and I was finally alone.

I opened my laptop, pulled up the full Award, and started reading. But I couldn't concentrate—the words kept dancing, my eyes skipping from paragraph to paragraph without retention. I needed to get home. I needed to read this properly.

I forwarded the Award to the three senior lawyers who'd fought beside me: *Review and comment. We won. Everything.*

The drive home passed in a blur. I kept replaying moments from the case—the bathroom eureka that had unravelled their entire claim, the tribunal's pattern of limiting our evidence while accommodating theirs, the institutional support that had evaporated with the new administration, the Special Assistant who hadn't. Twenty-five months I'd waited for this. Twenty-five months the tribunal had spent trying to find a way around the truth.

At home, I opened my laptop, pulled up the full Award, and started reading.

Ten pages in, my phone chimed.

Another email. Same sender. Same tribunal.

Different subject line: *Formal Complaint to the Legal Practitioners Disciplinary Committee.*

I stared at the screen.

I didn't open it. Not immediately. I sat there, laptop showing me victory, phone showing me... what? Retaliation? Punishment? The price?

When I finally opened the second email, my hands were no longer steady.

It was a summons—a formal disciplinary complaint filed against me by the three arbitrators. The charges were vague but damning in their implications: imputing bias to the tribunal, attacking the character and integrity of the arbitrators, discrediting the arbitral process, and making baseless corruption allegations.

I checked the date on both emails.

The Award: September 6, 2024, 2:47 PM. The summons: September 6, 2024, 3:16 PM.

Twenty-nine minutes.

They'd spent twenty-five months writing an Award they couldn't avoid, ruling in favour of the government because the evidence left them no choice, protecting their reputations as Senior Advocates of Nigeria. And then, twenty-nine minutes after delivering that Award, they'd filed a complaint designed to destroy mine.

I closed the laptop. Put down the phone. Sat in the silence of my study.

The dominant emotion wasn't anger. It wasn't even shocking. I'd known the tribunal was hostile—I'd formally challenged them for lack of independence and impartiality, documented concerning patterns in their conduct, raised questions about decisions that consistently favoured the Claimant. I'd expected consequences. What I hadn't expected was this: victory and retaliation delivered in the same afternoon, like two sides of the same coin.

But as I sat there, letting the reality settle over me, I realised something else.

I felt triumph.

Pure, uncomplicated triumph.

Because they'd had to rule in my favour. After everything—the pattern of decisions I'd documented, the concerning procedural conduct, the Company's claims I'd dismantled, the twenty-five-month delay—they'd had no choice. The evidence was too strong. The arguments were unassailable. They could pursue disciplinary action against me for challenging them, but they couldn't escape the power of the written words.

Three billion dollars saved for my country.

A bogus claim demolished.

A hostile tribunal cornered by the facts.

And all I'd done was my job. Defended my client with integrity. Challenged apparent lack of independence and impartiality when I saw it. Refused to be silenced or intimidated.

If that's what they wanted to retaliate against me for, so be it.

I picked up my phone and called the senior lawyer who'd become closest to me during the case. He answered on the first ring.

"Did you see it?" His voice was jubilant. "We won! Andy, we actually—"

"I saw it," I said. "Both of them."

"Both—what?"

"Recheck your email. The arbitrators filed a disciplinary complaint against me. Same day as the Award. Twenty-nine minutes later."

Silence on the other end. Then: "Those bastards."

"Yes."

"Are you alright?"

I considered the question. The facts were clear: I'd won a three-billion-dollar case and faced disciplinary proceedings as a result. The government had not responded to my letters. The arbitrators had initiated formal charges. The situation was what it was.

"I'm fine," I said. "Better than fine. We won. They had to admit it. Everything else is just... the price."

"The price?"

"Of doing the right thing. Of refusing to play along. Of standing up to a hostile tribunal." I looked at the summons on my screen. "They're making an example of me. To any other lawyer who might think about challenging arbitrators who abuse their authority."

"What are you going to do?"

"Fight it, of course. What else?" I smiled, though he couldn't see it. "I've fought everything else. Why stop now?"

We talked for a few more minutes, then I let him go to read the Award properly. I sat alone in my study as the afternoon light faded, looking at the two emails side by side.

Victory and punishment.

Vindication and retaliation.

The best and worst days of my professional life, delivered twenty-nine minutes apart.

That's when I remembered what the investor had said: *You should write a book about this.*

Maybe I should.

Maybe the case deserved to be told. Not for vindication, but for the record. So that others would understand the full cost of challenging institutional impropriety—and decide for themselves whether that cost was worth paying.

Maybe someone needed to hear that I'll do it anyway.

That I'd do it again.

That integrity has a price, but silence costs more.

So let me tell you how I got here. Let me take you back five years, to a phone call at Heathrow Airport, to a Friday morning in my bathroom, to a hostile tribunal, to counsel arrangements involving client offices that create apparent conflicts, and twenty-five months of silence. Let me show you what a bogus claim for three billion dollars looks like, and what it costs to stop it.

Let me show you the price of challenging a hostile tribunal.

* * * *

This is a true story and this account is based on my personal experience and recollections. To protect parties and ongoing legal matters, names and certain identifying details have been changed, omitted or redacted. The events as I experienced them are accurate to the best of my knowledge and belief. All statements reflect my observations and professional judgment during these proceedings.

I am still fighting the disciplinary complaint. The outcome remains uncertain. But my experience—what I observed and how I understood it—deserves to be told.

This is my account of what happened.

Chapter 1

The Call

Heathrow Airport has a particular quality of light in the late afternoon—filtered through glass and steel, simultaneously harsh and diffuse. I was sitting in the departure lounge for my connecting flight to New York, reviewing case files on my laptop, when my phone rang.

The number displayed was from Abuja. I didn't recognise it immediately, but the country code and area designation told me it was official—government or institutional. After over thirty years of practice, you develop instincts about these things.

"Andy Oji," I answered.

"Mr Oji, good afternoon." The voice was formal, professional. "This is a call from the Federal Government legal team. We understand you're currently travelling, but we have an urgent matter we'd like to discuss with you."

I closed my laptop. "I'm listening."

"We have a case that requires a specialist in international arbitration. It's... significant. Both in terms of the amounts involved and the nature of the dispute. We've been asking around, and your name came up repeatedly."

"What kind of case?"

There was a brief pause, as if he was choosing his words carefully. "Defence contract. It involves a private military contractor and a terminated contract related to national security operations. The matter has been referred to arbitration, and the Attorney General's office needs experienced counsel to represent the government's interests."

Defence contract. Private military contractor. National security. Arbitration. The combination was unusual enough to be interesting.

"What's the claim amount?" I asked.

"Substantial. We can provide full details once we meet, but we're talking about a figure that would have... considerable implications for the national budget."

In government legal work, "considerable implications for the national budget" was code for either tens of millions or hundreds of millions—possibly more.

"When do you need an answer?"

"We'd like to meet as soon as you're back in the country. The matter is time-sensitive. Procedural deadlines are approaching."

I glanced at my watch. My flight to New York was boarding in forty minutes. I had an arbitration hearing there that would take the better part of a week. Then back to Lagos.

"I'll be back Friday," I said. "We can meet early next week."

"That would be acceptable. We'll arrange a formal meeting at the offices of the National Security Adviser and the Attorney General."

That got my attention. Cases that involved both the NSA and the AG weren't routine contract disputes. This was something else.

"I'll make myself available," I said.

We exchanged a few more details—contact information, preliminary dates—and ended the call. I sat in the departure lounge, phone in hand, mind already turning over the possibilities.

Private military contractor. National security operations. Terminated contract. Arbitration.

It had all the ingredients of a complex, high-stakes dispute. The kind of case that tests everything you know about arbitration practice, evidence, strategy, and the law. The kind of case that, if you win, validates your entire career.

Or if you lose, it haunts you forever.

I opened my laptop again and tried to return to my New York case files. But my concentration was broken. I kept thinking about that phone call. About what kind of military contract would end up in arbitration. About why they needed a specialist.

At thirty years of practice, I'd seen most variations of international disputes. I'd represented clients in arbitrations under UNCITRAL Rules, ICC, LCIA, AAA/ICDR. I'd argued cases involving Swiss, New York, French, English, and Nigerian law. I'd gone up against some of the most prestigious law firms in the world—and won.

I was the Managing Partner and Head of International Arbitration at COSMOLAWS. I had served as general counsel to two major airlines, negotiating international contracts and resolving complex cross-border commercial disputes. In those roles, I was not only engaged in contract formation and dispute resolution, but also in the conduct of complex international commercial arbitrations—acting as both counsel and arbitrator across multiple jurisdictions and industries, including aviation, banking, construction, defence, energy, oil and gas, and telecommunications.

This was what I did. This was what I was good at.

But something about this case—even just the bare outline of it—felt different.

The boarding announcement for my New York flight came over the speakers. I packed up my laptop, gathered my carry-on, and joined the queue at the gate. But my mind was still in Abuja, still thinking about that call.

I had no way of knowing, standing in that departure lounge at Heathrow, that I'd just agreed to the most consequential case of my life. That the "substantial" claim would turn out to be US$3 billion. That the arbitrators would be hostile from the start and would display an apparent lack of independence and impartiality. That there will be counsel arrangements involving client offices that create apparent conflicts. That winning would take five years and threaten to cost me more than I could imagine.

If I'd known all that, would I have said yes?

I want to think I would have.

But in that moment, I didn't know. I just knew that something interesting had landed in my path, and I was curious enough to pursue it.

* * * *

The New York arbitration took six days. It was a complex joint venture dispute involving aircraft leasing and financing contracts—my speciality. The opposing counsel was a partner at a major Wall Street firm, the kind of lawyer who charged four figures an hour and had associates do most of his thinking for him. I'd faced his type before.

We won. Not a close victory either—a clear, decisive win on both the facts and the law. The tribunal deliberated for barely an hour after closing arguments.

But throughout that week, part of my mind was elsewhere. I kept thinking about the case waiting for me in Abuja. During breaks in the hearing, I'd find myself wondering about the details. What kind of military contract? What had gone wrong? Why arbitration instead of litigation? What was the contractor claiming?

On the flight back to Lagos, I tried to focus on the victory we'd just secured. My client was pleased. The case had been handled efficiently—the arbitrators were professionals, clearly independent and knowledgeable. But I couldn't stop my mind from jumping ahead to the unknown.

I've always been like this—drawn to puzzles, to complex problems that don't have obvious solutions. The law, at its best, is an intellectual exercise. You take a set of facts, apply legal principles, construct arguments, and either you're right or you're wrong. The elegance is in extracting the facts from witnesses, constructing the legal arguments and knowing at which procedural stage to deploy which argument. The satisfaction is in being right.

This new case promised to be a puzzle. A big one.

When I landed in Lagos on Friday evening, I had three messages on my phone. One was from my office, confirming meetings for the following week. One was from the New York arbitration client, thanking me for the excellent representation.

The third was from the government legal team, providing details for the meeting the following Monday at the National Security Adviser's office.

That weekend, I tried to relax. Tried to focus on family, on routine, on the hundred other matters that required my attention as Managing Partner of a busy law firm. But Monday kept approaching, and with it, the unknown.

Sunday evening, I sat in my study reviewing what little I knew. Private military contractor. National security operations. Terminated contract. Substantial claim. Arbitration.

Not much to go on. But enough to know it would be interesting.

I pulled out a fresh legal pad and wrote at the top: Military Contractor Arbitration - Initial Questions

Underneath, I listed what I needed to know:

- Who is the contractor?
- What was the nature of the contract?
- Why was it terminated?
- What is the contractor claiming?
- What evidence or legal theory was presented by the contractor?
- What's the government's position?
- Who are the arbitrators?
- What are the applicable rules and the procedural status?
- What's the timeline?

Basic questions. But until I had answers, everything else was speculation.

I set down my pen and looked at the blank page below my questions.

Five years from that moment, I'd be sitting in my study looking at two emails—one announcing victory, one summoning me to disciplinary proceedings. I'd be wondering if it had all been worth it.

But that Sunday evening, I didn't know any of that. I just knew I had a meeting Monday morning, and I was curious to find out what kind of case warranted meetings at both the NSA and AG's offices.

* * * *

Monday morning arrived clear and bright. I dressed carefully—dark suit, white shirt, understated tie. First impressions matter, even with government officials you're being hired by, especially with government officials.

The drive from Lagos to Abuja is roughly 8 hours, but I'd flown up the night before and stayed at a hotel near the meeting venue. I wanted to be sharp for the meeting, not exhausted from travel.

The National Security Adviser's office was in the Three Arms Zone—the heavily secured area of Abuja where the Presidential Villa, National Assembly, and Supreme Court are located. Getting through the multiple security checkpoints took time. They checked my identification, made phone calls, and verified my appointment. Eventually, I was cleared through and directed to a building complex that housed several government offices.

Inside, the atmosphere was what I'd expected—institutional, bureaucratic, quietly efficient. People moved with purpose through corridors decorated with official photographs and Nigerian flags. I was shown to a conference room and asked to wait.

I sat down, placed my briefcase on the table, and took in my surroundings. The room was standard government issue—long table, adequate chairs, water pitchers, and glasses. Nothing fancy. This was a working space, not somewhere designed to impress.

The door opened, and four people entered.

The first was a military officer in uniform—the Principal Staff Officer to the National Security Adviser. He carried himself with the bearing of someone who'd spent a career in command positions. We shook hands.

The second introduced himself as the Special Assistant to the NSA (Legal). He was younger, sharp-eyed, with the quick energy of someone who'd risen through civil service ranks on merit rather than connections. There was something in his manner—an alertness, an intensity—that I immediately recognised. This was someone who cared not just about procedures and protocols, but about doing things right.

The third was from the Attorney General's office—the Director of Civil Litigation. Older, measured, with the careful diction of someone who'd spent decades navigating government bureaucracy.

The fourth was another lawyer from the AG's office, whose role seemed to be primarily support and documentation.

We all sat down. Coffee was offered and declined all around. This was business.

The Principal Staff Officer began. "Mr Oji, thank you for coming on short notice. We have a situation that requires experienced counsel, and your reputation precedes you."

I nodded. "I'm here to help in whatever way I can."

"The case involves a private military contractor—we'll call them the Company for now—who was engaged by the Federal Government to conduct covert military operations against insurgent forces in the Northeast. The contract was substantial. The operation was critical to national security. Things did not go as planned."

He paused, and the Special Assistant picked up the narrative.

"The Company claims they were terminated improperly. They've filed a claim for approximately US$3 billion in arbitration. They say they procured military hardware, recruited and trained personnel, executed the contract, and were then forced out of the country without full payment. They claim breach of contract and asserted that the settlement agreement was obtained by duress."

Three billion. The number hung in the air.

"And your position?" I asked.

"Our position is that the contract was terminated by mutual agreement. There was a settlement agreement. Both parties signed it. The Company sent us a letter of appreciation. We thought the matter was closed. Now, years later, they've filed this arbitration claim for approximately three billion U.S. dollars."

I wrote down the figure. Three billion. An extraordinary sum.

"What's the basis of their claim?"

"They say they procured military hardware—helicopter gunships, armoured tanks, other equipment. They say they recruited and trained foreign personnel. They say they executed the contract but were forced out of the country without full payment. They're claiming for equipment they say was confiscated, for lease rental fees, for cost overruns, for damages, and for pre- and post- interest. The claim is comprehensive."

"And your view of these claims?"

The Special Assistant spoke up. "We believe the claim is without merit. But we need experienced counsel to demonstrate that. The Company has sophisticated lawyers. They've submitted extensive documentation. We need someone who can analyse their case and build our defence."

I pulled out my legal pad and began taking notes. "What's the status of the arbitration?"

"It was filed after a Federal High Court matter. The court directed the parties to arbitration. The tribunal has been constituted. Procedural orders have been issued. We've filed preliminary responses, but we need experienced arbitration counsel to take over the case."

"Who handled it at the Federal High Court?"

"We did," the Director said, gesturing to himself and his colleague. "Our office. We thought the settlement agreement would be dispositive. But the Company's strategy appears to be to set aside the settlement and pursue the full claim."

I wrote: Settlement agreement - key defence?

"What evidence do you have?"

The Special Assistant spoke up. "We have the contract. We have payment records showing funds transferred to the Company. We have correspondence. We have the settlement agreement. What we don't have is full cooperation from all the government personnel who were involved in the original operation. Some have been... unavailable."

"Unavailable how?"

There was a pause. The Principal Staff Officer said carefully, "Some are facing other legal matters. Some have been dismissed from service. Some have declined to participate. It's... complicated."

I understood immediately. This wasn't just a legal case. This was a case where the institutional memory and witness availability had been compromised by time, politics, and perhaps corruption.

"What about the Company's evidence?"

"They've submitted Notice of Arbitration, a brief description of the claim, volumes of documents. Two cartons' worth, in addition to other information. We've reviewed them, but candidly, we need someone with your expertise to analyse the case properly."

"And the arbitrators?"

"Three arbitrators under the UNCITRAL Rules. All Senior Advocates. All experienced in commercial arbitration."

That should have been reassuring. Senior Advocates—the highest designation for lawyers in Nigeria—serving as arbitrators under established international rules. But something in the way it was said caught my attention.

"Any concerns about the tribunal?"

The four officials exchanged glances. The Special Assistant said, "Not at this time. The proceedings are just beginning."

Which wasn't quite an answer. I made a mental note to revisit that question later.

We spent the next hour going through details—procedural history, timeline, upcoming deadlines. They provided me with copies of the court file, the settlement agreement, and preliminary submissions. Two cardboard boxes of documents sat in the corner—the Company's evidence, they said. I'd need to review all of it.

Finally, the Principal Staff Officer said, "Mr Oji, we need someone who can handle this case at the highest level. Someone who understands both the legal complexities and the national security sensitivities. We've made inquiries. Your name came up repeatedly. Will you take the case?"

I looked at the four men sitting across from me. Government officials doing their best to protect national interests with inadequate resources and compromised witnesses. A three-billion-dollar claim that could devastate the national budget. A private military contractor with sophisticated lawyers and a comprehensive litigation strategy.

And me, being asked to step into the middle of it.

In my career, I'd won cases against New York lawyers arguing New York law. I'd beaten English barristers on English law. I'd prevailed against Swiss firms under Swiss law and against French firms under French law. I'd handled billion-dollar disputes across multiple jurisdictions and industries.

But three billion dollars. For the government. With national security implications.

If I won, I'd save my country a staggering sum. If I lost...

I didn't finish that thought.

"Yes," I said. "I'll take the case."

The Special Assistant smiled—the first genuine smile I'd seen in the meeting. "Thank you. We'll arrange the formal appointment through the Attorney General's office."

We shook hands all around. They gave me the boxes of documents, the case files, and contact information for further coordination. I left the building with my arms full of paper and my head full of questions.

As I drove back to my hotel, I thought about what I'd just committed to. Five years of arbitration. Hostile witnesses or no witnesses at all. A sophisticated opponent with unlimited resources. Three billion dollars at stake.

And somewhere in those two boxes of documents, there had to be a defence—some angle, some argument, some piece of evidence that would unravel the Company's claim.

I just had to find it.

I didn't know yet about the eureka moment that would come one Friday morning in my bathroom. I didn't know about the hostile tribunal, the fabricated records, the distorted and unsupported arguments, the twenty-five-month wait. I didn't know what the price would be for winning.

I just knew I had work to do.

And I was looking forward to it.

Chapter 2

The Appointment

The formal letter arrived three days after my meeting at the National Security Adviser's office. It was dated June 27, 2019, and bore the reference number MJ/CIV/ABJ/ARBT/-/19. The letterhead was from the Office of the Attorney General of the Federation, and the language was appropriately bureaucratic:

You are hereby appointed to represent the Federal Government of Nigeria in the arbitration proceedings instituted by [the Company]. You are directed to liaise with the Office of the National Security Adviser to obtain the facts and materials necessary for the defence of the nation's interests.

I read it twice, then filed it carefully. This wasn't just another engagement letter. This was authority from the chief legal officer of the Federal Government. Whatever happened in this case—victory or defeat—it would be on the record that I had been formally entrusted with defending three billion dollars of the nation's resources. It was a huge responsibility, and I resolved to defend the country to the hilt.

The weight of that settled over me as I sat in my office that afternoon. Three billion dollars. Not three million, not three hundred million. Three billion. The kind of number that makes the news, that affects budgets, that can define or destroy careers.

I picked up the phone and called my senior lawyers into my office—the three who would form the core team for this case. They arrived within minutes and took seats around my conference table.

"The formal appointment came through," I said, sliding copies of the letter across to them. "We're officially counsel for the Federal Government in the arbitration. Three billion dollars at stake."

One of them—the lawyer who would eventually become closest to me during this case—let out a low whistle as he read the appointment letter. "It's official then."

"It's official," I confirmed. "And we have work to do. The tribunal has ordered the Company to submit its statement of claim within thirty days. While we wait for that, we need to analyse everything the government has already provided—the Federal High Court file, the settlement agreement, all the documents from the initial proceedings."

I'd already reviewed the materials once, but it was a preliminary scan. Now we needed a systematic analysis. We needed to understand not only what the Company had claimed in the Federal High Court, but also why the court directed arbitration rather than proceeding with those claims. We needed to understand the settlement agreement inside and out. We needed to know this case better than anyone else in the room when the arbitration hearing eventually came.

"How do you want to divide the work?" one of the lawyers asked.

"I'll take the overall strategy and case theory. You three focus on different aspects—one on the contract documents and settlement agreement, one on the procedural history and Federal High Court record, and one on legal research. We'll meet daily to coordinate and share findings."

They nodded, already making notes.

"One more thing," I said. "The government officials mentioned that some witnesses may not be available. Personnel have moved on, some are dealing with other issues, and some don't want to be involved. That means we need to build this defence primarily on documentary evidence. Which means we need to know every document, every detail, every date. Nothing can surprise us."

We spent the next hour reviewing what we had. The Federal High Court file was comprehensive—the Company's initial claim, the government's response based on the settlement agreement, and the court's ruling directing the matter to arbitration. Reading through it, I could see the outline of the Company's strategy: they argued that the settlement was invalid, obtained under duress, and not an actual meeting of minds.

But the documents told a different story. The settlement agreement was professionally drafted, signed by authorised representatives, and properly executed. More importantly, there was the letter—the Company's own letter, sent after the settlement was signed, thanking the government and expressing satisfaction with the resolution.

That letter was going to be crucial.

"This should be straightforward," one of my team said, reading through the settlement file. "They signed an agreement. They thanked the government afterwards. How can they now claim it was obtained through duress?"

"Because claims of this magnitude invite revisionist narratives," I said. "And because they have sophisticated lawyers who will try to create doubt where none should exist. Our job is to make the truth so clear, so well-documented, that no tribunal can ignore it."

* * * *

The following week, I returned to Abuja to meet with the Special Assistant at the NSA's office. The appointment letter had directed me to coordinate with the NSA for facts and materials, and I needed to establish a working relationship and understand what support would be available.

The Special Assistant met me in a working conference room—smaller and less formal than where our first meeting had been held. Maps hung on the walls, and files were stacked on shelves. This was where the actual work of government happened.

"Mr Oji," he said, shaking my hand. "Thank you for taking this case. I want to be completely honest with you about what we're facing."

I appreciated the directness. "Please."

He sat down across from me. "The operation itself was highly classified. The contract with the Company was for the procurement of military hardware and the provision of personnel to conduct covert, asymmetrical warfare against the insurgents. Time was critical—we needed to act quickly based on intelligence about insurgent locations."

"What happened?"

"Things didn't go according to plan," he said carefully. "I don't have all the technical details—many of the personnel who were directly involved are no longer available to us. But I know that eventually the contract was terminated by mutual agreement. Both parties signed a settlement agreement. The Company sent us a letter of appreciation, thanking us for how the matter was handled."

"And now they're claiming three billion dollars."

His expression darkened. "Now they're claiming the settlement was obtained through coercion. They're claiming they're owed money for equipment, services, and various costs. All the details will be in their statement of claim when they file it with the tribunal."

"What can you tell me about the merits of their claims?"

He spread his hands. "Honestly? I don't have enough detailed knowledge of exactly what was delivered, what was paid, and all the contract terms. That's why we need you. The documents exist—payment records, correspondence, and contract files. But we need someone who can analyse it all and build the defence. Someone who understands international arbitration."

"What about witnesses? Will you be able to provide people who can testify about what happened?"

"That's going to be difficult," he admitted. "Some of the key personnel have moved on, some are dealing with other issues, some simply don't want to be involved. We'll do what we can, but you shouldn't count on extensive witness testimony from our side."

This was concerning but not unexpected. Government cases often had this problem: turnover, reluctance to testify, and loss of institutional memory.

"Then we'll build the defence primarily on documents," I said. "Which means I need access to everything you have. Payment records, authorisations, correspondence, contract files, everything."

"I'll get you what we have." He pulled out a folder and handed it to me. "This is a start. Payment authorisations, some correspondence, and initial contract documents. There's more in the archives, but it will take time to compile."

I opened the folder and scanned the contents. Bank transfers. Authorisation memos. Email chains. The documentary foundation of a government contract.

"One more thing," the Special Assistant said, his voice taking on a different tone. "I want you to know that you have my full support in this case. Whatever you need, whatever access I can provide, you'll have it. This matters, Mr Oji. The Company didn't perform as contracted. They're now trying to use arbitration to extract money they're not entitled to. We can't let that succeed."

I looked at him across the table. In a case where so many people seemed to want to distance themselves from the matter, here was someone who understood what was at stake. Someone who cared about doing the right thing.

"Thank you," I said. "That means a great deal."

We spent another hour reviewing what he could provide—contact information for personnel who might be available, procedures for accessing archived files, and protocols for handling classified information. By the time I left, I had a clearer sense of both the support available and its limitations.

I would have documentary evidence. I would have the Special Assistant's cooperation. But I would be building this defence largely on paper, not testimony.

Which meant those documents had to be unassailable.

* * * *

Back in Lagos, I assembled my team and laid out the situation. We had the Federal High Court record, the settlement agreement, initial documents from the NSA, and more materials on the way. The Company would file its arbitration claim soon, within the 30 days ordered by the tribunal.

"Until they file, we work with what we have," I said. "The Federal High Court record shows us their basic approach. They'll likely expand on it for the arbitration, but the core strategy will be the same—invalidate the settlement, claim they weren't paid for work performed, demand three billion dollars."

"How long do we have until they file?" one lawyer asked.

"Thirty days from the tribunal's order. Which means we have a few weeks to get ahead of them. I want us to understand the settlement agreement fully. I want to know every payment that was made. I want to timeline everything so that when their claim arrives, we can immediately identify any misstatements or distortions."

We established a routine. Morning sessions reviewing documents. Afternoon sessions on legal research. Evening sessions synthesising what we'd learned. Every day, we build our understanding of the case.

The settlement agreement became our focus. It was the cornerstone of the defence—proof that the parties had resolved their dispute, that both sides had agreed to the terms, that the matter was closed. If we could establish that the settlement was valid and voluntary, the Company's three-billion-dollar claim would collapse.

I read the settlement agreement dozens of times. The language was clear: both parties agreed to terminate the contract by mutual consent, to settle all outstanding obligations, and to release each other from further claims. The signatures were authentic, the execution proper.

And then there was the letter—the Company's letter of appreciation, sent after the settlement was signed. I must have read it fifty times, memorising every word.

We wish to express our appreciation for the professional manner in which this matter has been resolved...

Professional manner. Appreciation. These were not the words of a party that had been coerced or forced into an unfair settlement. These were the words of a party satisfied with the outcome.

That letter was going to win this case. I was certain of it.

* * * *

Three weeks passed. January 30, 2020, arrived—the deadline for the Company to file its statement of claim.

Nothing arrived.

I waited a few days, assuming there might be administrative delays—still nothing.

On February 28, I wrote to the tribunal: We note that the Claimant has failed to submit its statement of claim as ordered. We request guidance on how the tribunal wishes to proceed.

The tribunal's response came shortly after. They'd granted the Company an extension to March 9, 2020. No explanation provided. No requirement that the Company had applied for the extension before the deadline passed. Just... more time.

I frowned when I read the email. Under the UNCITRAL Arbitration Rules 2013, the statement of claim should be submitted within a time period determined by the tribunal—in this case, thirty days. The Rules are deliberately designed this way: arbitration exists as an alternative to litigation specifically because it promises speed and efficiency. Time limits are kept short to serve that purpose.

The tribunal may extend those time periods, but the Rules contemplate that a party seeking extension would show "sufficient cause." That meant applying before the deadline passes, explaining why more time is needed, giving the other party notice and opportunity to respond.

The Company had done none of that. They'd simply missed the deadline. And the tribunal had granted an extension anyway—without any application, without any stated justification, without consulting us.

This undermined the fundamental purpose of arbitration's time limits: to ensure the process moves efficiently toward resolution.

I made a note in my file: *Extension granted without application, without justification, without notice to respondent. Monitor this pattern.*

* * * *

March 9, 2020, arrived. The extended deadline. Again, no submission from the Company.

I wrote to the tribunal again, pointing out that the extended deadline had also passed. This time, no response.

Then, on April 1, 2020, the tribunal issued a new procedural order. The deadline for the Company's submission was now April 7.

My team and I discussed this in our daily meeting. "They're being very accommodating to the Company," one lawyer observed.

"Perhaps too accommodating," I said. "But we don't challenge the tribunal over procedural matters. Not yet. We focus on being ready whenever they finally file."

* * * *

April 7 came and went. No submission. Again.

But something else happened that week. The COVID-19 pandemic, which had been worsening throughout March, reached Lagos. The Lagos State government issued a mandatory lockdown order. All businesses closed. Movement restricted. No one could go to the offices.

I was working from home when the tribunal's next email arrived. They'd granted the Company yet another extension—to May 1.

But the second part of the order stopped me cold: our time for filing our statement of defence would continue to run despite the lockdown.

I read that twice, not quite believing it.

The Company, which had now missed three deadlines over three months, was getting a fourth extension. But we—unable to access our offices, our files, our staff, our witnesses during a government-mandated lockdown—were expected to file our defence on schedule.

The lockdown meant I couldn't get to the office where all our organised files were. I couldn't meet with my team in person. I couldn't access the physical documents we'd been working with. Lagos was completely shut down—not like a holiday or non-business day, but a security emergency with restricted movement.

And the tribunal considered this equivalent to a weekend.

I drafted a response immediately, requesting that our filing deadline be suspended during the lockdown. I explained the situation—government-ordered closure, inability to access materials, unprecedented circumstances.

The tribunal's response was brief: the lockdown would be treated as a non-business day. Our deadline will continue to run.

I sat at my home office, looking at that email, and felt the first real stirring of concern about this tribunal.

The pattern was now unmistakable. The UNCITRAL Rules require the statement of claim to be filed within a defined period—in this case, thirty days—precisely to ensure arbitration delivers on its core promise: speed. Parties choose arbitration over litigation specifically to avoid endless delays.

Under those same Rules, tribunals have discretion to extend time periods where parties show "sufficient cause." The Company had shown no cause—they'd simply missed their thirty-day deadline, then missed it again, and again, without explanation or advance notice. Yet they'd received four extensions over four months. They'd been given more than 120 days to file what the Rules contemplated should take 30.

We had shown extraordinary cause—a government-mandated pandemic lockdown that made it physically impossible to access our offices and files. Yet we were denied any accommodation, our deadline continuing to run as if nothing had happened.

This wasn't discretion. This was differential treatment. The same Rules, designed to ensure speed and efficiency, applied differently depending on which party needed accommodation. One party got four months to do what should take one month. The other party was expected to work through a global pandemic as if it were a weekend.

This was the first moment I questioned the tribunal's procedural balance.

But I said nothing yet. I couldn't challenge the tribunal over this without seeming petty or obstructionist. And besides, we'd been working hard. We had our analysis complete. We could file our defence despite the obstacles.

The Incomplete Submission

On May 1, 2020—five months after the original deadline—the Company finally submitted something.

But what arrived wasn't a proper statement of claim. It was unsigned and incomplete, accompanied by an application for more time.

Over the next several days, they submitted their case in pieces:

- May 3: A bundle of exhibits
- May 6: A signed version of the statement of claim—still incomplete
- Unsigned and unsworn witness statements

I read through what they'd filed with growing concern. This wasn't how arbitration worked. Under UNCITRAL Rules, the statement of claim must be complete and properly executed when filed.

But more troubling than the piecemeal submission was what was missing. Article 20(2) of the UNCITRAL Arbitration Rules, 2013—the rules governing this arbitration—sets out specific requirements for a statement of claim. It must include:

(a) The names and contact details of the parties (b) A statement of the facts supporting the claim (c) The points at issue (d) The relief or remedy sought (e) The legal grounds or arguments supporting the claim.

The Company's submission included the facts and the relief sought. But subsection (e)—the legal grounds and arguments—was completely absent. They'd filed bare allegations without explaining the legal basis for their three-billion-dollar claim.

This wasn't a minor technicality. The requirement is to provide the respondent with sufficient information to prepare an effective defence.

Without knowing the legal theories supporting the claim, how could we respond adequately?

It was, effectively, a setup for trial by ambush.

* * * *

On May 15 and 18, the Company submitted two applications to the tribunal:

1. An order deeming their unsworn witness statements as properly submitted, with the opportunity to swear them at a later date

2. An order amending Procedural Order No. 1 by deleting the requirement to file legal grounds and arguments with the statement of claim.

I drafted our objection carefully. The Company was asking the tribunal to waive a mandatory requirement of the UNCITRAL Rules—not a procedural preference, but a formal requirement that couldn't be dispensed with.

I wrote:

The Claimant has submitted an incomplete statement of claim that fails to comply with Article 20(2)(e) of the UNCITRAL Arbitration Rules, 2013. The requirement to include legal grounds and arguments is not discretionary. It is a mandatory formal requirement designed to ensure a fair process and prevent ambush.

The respondent objects to any waiver of this requirement. The Claimant should be ordered to submit a complete statement of claim in accordance with the Rules, including all legal grounds and arguments supporting their claim.

Without this information, the respondent's ability to prepare an effective defence is severely hampered. We cannot respond to legal theories that have not been disclosed.

I submitted the objection and waited for the tribunal's response.

The Tribunal's Ruling

The ruling came in early June.

The tribunal accepted the Company's incomplete statement of claim as correctly submitted. They waived the requirement under Article 20(2)(e). The Company would not be required to provide its legal grounds and arguments in advance.

They also deemed the unsigned, unsworn witness statements as properly filed, with permission to formalise them later.

The tribunal extended the same accommodation to us, even though we hadn't requested it and didn't need it.

But then came the truly absurd part.

The tribunal ruled that our time for filing the statement of defence would begin running from May 1, 2020—the date of the Company's first incomplete submission.

Not from May 3, when they submitted the exhibit bundle.

Not from May 6, when they finally submitted a signed version—still incomplete.

Not from the date of the ruling.

Not from when they actually provided everything we needed to respond.

From May 1. When they'd submitted an unsigned, incomplete document that didn't comply with the Rules.

I stared at the ruling. We were given 30 days to respond—but those 30 days had already started counting from a date when we didn't even have the complete statement of claim to respond to.

The Company took 5 months to submit documents piecemeal over multiple dates. The tribunal had accommodated every delay. But when it came to our defence deadline, they'd started the clock from the earliest possible date—before we'd even received everything we needed to respond.

It was procedural sleight of hand. The Company got five months and multiple extensions. We got less than thirty days—probably less than 15 days because the clock had started running while their submission was still incomplete.

I called my team on a video conference.

"They've just waived a mandatory requirement of the UNCITRAL Rules," I said. "Not a discretionary procedural matter. A formal requirement that exists precisely to prevent what's about to happen—we'll go into the hearing not knowing the legal basis of their three-billion-dollar claim."

"Can they do that?" one of my lawyers asked.

"They just did," I said. "And they've started our defence clock from May 1, even though we didn't receive their complete submission until days later. We have less time than the Rules provide because they're counting from an incomplete submission."

"That's absurd," someone said.

"It is," I agreed. "And this pattern will be important to document."

I looked at my team. "The Company missed four deadlines over five months to file their statement of claim. When they finally filed, it was incomplete and didn't comply with the Rules. We objected. The tribunal waived the requirement and started our defence deadline from their first incomplete submission—giving us less time to respond."

"Meanwhile," I continued, "we were ordered to file our defence during a government-mandated lockdown, with no access to our offices, and told that the pandemic was equivalent to a weekend."

"What do we do?" someone asked.

In my career, I'd won cases against New York lawyers arguing New York law. I'd beaten English barristers on English law. I'd prevailed against Swiss firms under Swiss law and against French firms under French law. I'd handled billion-dollar disputes across multiple jurisdictions and industries.

"We file our defence," I said. "Complete. On time. Properly executed. In full compliance with every requirement of the Rules. We don't give them any basis to rule against us on procedural grounds."

"And then?"

"And then we document everything. Every accommodation they give to the Company. Every obstacle they place in our way. Every deviation from proper procedure. Because if this pattern continues—and I believe it will—we may need to challenge the tribunal formally."

* * * *

We had less than thirty days to file our statement of defence. Working from home, coordinating by phone and email, pulling together documents we'd fortunately digitised, we prepared and filed our defence within the tribunal's deadline.

We filed our statement of defence within fifteen days. Complete. On time. Properly executed. Including our legal grounds and arguments, as required by Article 20(2)(e)—even though the Company hadn't been required to do the same.

Despite the lockdown. Despite being unable to access our office. Despite the double standard.

Because that's what the tribunal had ordered.

And because I wasn't going to give them any basis to rule against us on procedural grounds.

The Scorecard

I kept a running tally in my notes:

The Company:

- Original deadline: January 30, 2020
- First extension (granted without application): March 9, 2020
- Second extension: April 7, 2020
- Third extension: May 1, 2020
- Finally submitted: May 1-6, 2020 (piecemeal, unsigned, incomplete)
- Total delay: Approximately 5 months
- Penalty: None
- Consequence: Waiver of mandatory Rule requirements

The Respondent:

- Deadline: March 16, 2020 (later adjusted due to the Company's delays)
- Requested extension due to government-mandated pandemic lockdown: Denied

- Lockdown treated as: "Non-business day" equivalent to a weekend
- Filed: On time, complete, in full compliance with all Rules

The pattern was already clear. And this was only the statement of claim.

I didn't know it yet, but the Company's reply to our defence—due in 15 days—would take them more than twelve months to file. And the tribunal would accommodate that delay just as readily as they'd accommodated these.

Altogether, the Company would take approximately 18 months to submit the filings they were required to submit under the Rules within 45 days. And the tribunal would grant every extension requested without cogent reasons.

* * * *

Now it was the Company's turn to file its reply. They had fifteen days from the date they received our defence—a deadline of July 22, 2020.

I wondered how long it would actually take them.

And I wondered if the tribunal would hold them to the deadline.

Based on what I'd observed so far, I had my doubts.

Chapter 3

The Analysis

The Company's reply to our defence was due on July 22, 2020. After that, we would have fifteen days to file our rejoinder—our response to their reply.

But the Company's reply still hadn't arrived.

But I couldn't wait for them to file before beginning my analysis. The Company's statement of claim, filed in May 2020 after five months of delays, had included two cartons' worth of exhibits. Their reply—whenever it finally came—would add more. I needed to understand their case completely before I could respond effectively.

So, in July 2020, I established a routine that would continue for the next eight months.

Eight a.m., before the demands of managing a law firm and handling other cases took over: three hours dedicated exclusively to the Company's case. Reading documents. Taking notes. Building timelines. Understanding the strategy behind their claim.

Then the work day—client meetings, court appearances, administrative duties, the hundred other matters that required attention. Other cases that couldn't be neglected just because this one was massive.

The evening. Six p.m. to nine p.m.: another three hours on the case. Every single day. Weekends included.

My team followed the same discipline. We'd divided the work—one lawyer focused on analysing the contract documents and payment records, another on the Company's allegations and evidence, the third on legal research and applicable law. But we all read everything. We all understood the whole picture.

Because this case was going to be won or lost on the details.

The Reply That Took Twelve Months

According to the tribunal's procedural timetable, the Company had fifteen days from July 8, 2020, to file its reply to our statement of defence. The deadline was July 22, 2020.

July 22 came and went—no reply filed.

By now, I recognised the pattern. After what had happened with the statement of claim—five months of delays, four missed deadlines, and a waiver of mandatory Rule requirements—I knew better than to expect the tribunal to enforce this deadline either.

But I wrote to them anyway, noting that the deadline had passed and requesting guidance.

No response.

August passed. September. October. The silence stretched on.

By November 2020, four months after the deadline, I was tracking the delay in my activity log with grim fascination. Would they take as long to reply as they did with the statement of claim? Longer?

The answer, it turned out, was longer.

* * * *

On March 19, 2021—eight months after the deadline—the Company finally submitted something: an application seeking an extension of time to file their reply.

Not the reply itself. An application asking for more time. Eight months late.

The application offered no compelling explanation for the delay. No force majeure. No unforeseen circumstances. Just a request for more time, submitted long after any reasonable tribunal would have considered the party in default.

I drafted our response immediately. We objected. We pointed out that the Company had now established a clear pattern: miss deadlines, wait months, then apply for extensions after the fact. We noted that this was the same pattern that had governed the statement of claim, where they'd taken five months to file a document due in thirty days.

We requested that the tribunal, at a minimum, impose some consequence for the systematic disregard of procedural orders. A cost sanction. A direction that no further extensions would be granted. Something to indicate that deadlines had meaning.

The tribunal granted the extension to April 5, 2021.

The Company's own requested deadline. No consequence. No sanction. No comment on the eight-month delay.

* * * *

April 5, 2021, arrived.

I checked my email throughout the day, curious to see whether the Company would meet even its own proposed deadline.

They did not.

April 6. April 7. April 8. Nothing.

Weeks passed. I wrote to the tribunal again, noting that the Company had now missed the extended deadline they themselves had requested. Surely this merited some response?

Nothing.

May turned to June. June turned to July.

* * * *

On July 9, 2021, the Company finally submitted their reply—more than twelve months after the original deadline. Twelve clear months. Not days. Not weeks. An entire year.

They filed it in pieces, just as they'd done with the statement of claim. The reply on July 9. Supporting documents on July 12. Another bundle of exhibits on July 12.

I reviewed what they'd submitted with a sense of weary inevitability. The tribunal would accept it, just as they'd accepted everything else the Company had filed late, incomplete, or improperly.

And I was right.

No comment from the tribunal. No acknowledgement of the twelve-month delay. No consequence whatsoever.

The Company had been required to file two documents under the procedural schedule: a statement of claim (30 days) and a reply (15 days). Total time allocated: 45 days.

Time they'd actually taken: approximately eighteen months.

And the tribunal had accommodated every day of it.

* * * *

I updated my running tally:

The Company - Reply to Statement of Defence:

- Original deadline: July 22, 2020
- Months of silence: 8 months
- Extension application filed: March 19, 2021 (8 months late)
- Extended deadline granted: April 5, 2021
- Missed extended deadline: April 5, 2021 (no filing)
- Finally submitted: July 9-12, 2021 (piecemeal)
- Total delay: 12 months
- Penalty: None
- Consequence: Accepted without comment

Combined totals for Statement of Claim and Reply:

- Time allocated by Rules: 45 days total
- Time actually taken: Approximately 18 months
- Number of missed deadlines: At least 7
- Number of extensions granted: Multiple
- Number of sanctions imposed: Zero

* * * *

I called my team together after the reply finally arrived.

"They've done it again," I said. "Twelve months to file a document due in fifteen days. And the tribunal has accepted it without comment, just as they accepted the statement of claim five months late."

"This is systematic," one of my lawyers said. "Not occasional accommodation. Not reasonable flexibility. But a pattern of decisions consistently favouring one party."

"Yes," I agreed. "And we're documenting all of it. Because at some point, we'll need to make a formal challenge. We're going to need to show that this tribunal lacks the independence and impartiality required under the UNCITRAL Rules."

Another lawyer asked, "When do we challenge them?"

I'd been thinking about that. Challenging a tribunal is serious. It can appear obstructionist. It can antagonise arbitrators whose goodwill you might need. It's not something you do lightly or prematurely.

But it's also not something you delay too long, or you risk waiving your right to object.

"Soon," I said. "We're gathering evidence. When we challenge them, we need to show a pattern so clear, so systematic, so undeniable that no reasonable observer could dispute it."

"Do we have that yet?"

I looked at my notes. The eighteen-month delay for two simple documents. The waiver of mandatory Rule requirements. The denial of our extension requests during a pandemic, while granting theirs repeatedly without cause.

"We're getting there," I said. "We're very close." "We're approaching the point where the procedural pattern becomes undeniable."

I paused, then added, more carefully, "At this point, we can't know why the delays keep occurring. We can only observe that they are occurring, repeatedly, and always in one direction."

"There are several possible explanations," I continued. "It may be simple disorganisation. It may be that the Company was reassessing its strategy in light of the defence we filed. It may be that internal approvals were slow or that settlement was being considered. It may be some combination of all of these."

I looked down at my notes. "What matters is not the motive, which we cannot prove, but the effect. Whatever the reason, the tribunal has permitted a party to take twelve months to file a pleading due in fifteen days, without consequence. And that is not neutral case management."

One of the lawyers nodded. "So we don't argue why they delayed."

"Exactly," I said. "We don't speculate about intent. We document the pattern. We let the record speak for itself."

I continued. "From a defence perspective, the reply raised no new factual material capable of answering the settlement agreement we relied on, which made the length of the delay all the more striking."

Analysing Their Case

Their reply was aggressive. They doubled down on every allegation. They claimed new theories. They submitted more exhibits.

And they provided something we hadn't seen before: a detailed breakdown of their three-billion-dollar claim. But nothing new on the settlement agreement.

I read through it carefully, making notes during my morning and evening analysis sessions.

The Company's three-billion-dollar claim was comprehensive and ambitious. Equipment, fees, lease payments, cost overruns, damages, and escalating interest. It was designed to extract maximum value from every angle:

First, they claimed the balance of the full contract amount—the unpaid milestone payments for Stages Two through Five. They alleged they had performed the contract, but the government had refused to pay.

Second, they claimed the monetary value of military equipment they said belonged to them: helicopters, armoured vehicles (the REVA MRAPs), weapons, and ammunition. They alleged the government had "confiscated" or "appropriated" their property without compensation.

Third, they claimed lease rental fees for equipment they said had been deployed—helicopters, vehicles, night vision equipment, and communications equipment. These lease payments, they argued, were due for the proposed six-month contract duration.

Fourth, they claimed cost overruns—additional expenses allegedly incurred during the operation that exceeded the contract budget.

Fifth, they claimed damages for wrongful termination, asserting the government had breached the contract by forcing them out before completion.

Finally, they layered on interest: pre-award interest calculated from the "inception of the obligation"—from the moment they claimed each payment became due—and post-award interest that would continue accruing "until full liquidation," meaning until every dollar was paid.

Equipment value, unpaid fees, lease payments, overruns, damages, and compounding interest. It was a claim structured to grow larger with every passing month.

And as I read through their own supporting documents, I began to see something interesting.

The evidence they submitted to prove their claims... didn't actually prove what they thought it did.

Take the lease rental fees. They were claiming millions of dollars for equipment they said had been leased for the operation. But their own shipping manifests showed delivery dates that were after the contract had been terminated. If the equipment arrived after termination, how could they claim rental fees for its use during the operation?

Or the confiscated equipment claims. They said the government had seized their property without payment. But their own correspondence showed the government had provided clearances for the Company to repatriate equipment. And payment records showed the government had purchased certain equipment at agreed prices.

The more I read their evidence, the more contradictions I found. Documents that undermined their claims rather than supporting them. Timelines that didn't match their narrative. Correspondence that proved the opposite of what they were arguing.

I called my team together one evening in late July 2021.

"I think they've made a mistake," I said. "A big one."

"What kind of mistake?" one of them asked.

"They've submitted everything. Every document they have, trying to overwhelm us with volume. But they didn't analyse their own evidence carefully enough. Because much of what they've given us actually supports our defence, not their claim."

The lawyer who'd become closest to me during this case leaned forward. "Give me an example."

"Lease rental fees. They're claiming the equipment was used in the operation, so they're entitled to fees. But look at the shipping dates." I pulled out a chronology we'd prepared. "Equipment ordered in January, supposed to arrive in February. Actually arrived in May, after the contract was terminated in April. How can they claim rental fees for equipment that wasn't even there?"

"Maybe they're claiming it was there earlier?"

"Then where are the shipping records showing earlier delivery? They're not in their own exhibits. What they've given us proves late delivery or non-delivery. They've documented their own failure to perform."

Another lawyer spoke up. "So what's our strategy?"

"We use their own evidence against them. We show that, according to their own documents, they failed to deliver the equipment on time. We show that by their own correspondence, they acknowledged problems and delays. We show, by their own records, that the settlement was fair and voluntary. We use their evidence to prove our case."

"That's brilliant," someone said.

"It's not brilliant. It's just careful analysis. They submitted volumes of documents, hoping we wouldn't read them all carefully. We're going to prove we know their case better than they do."

The Rejoinder

We had fifteen days to file our rejoinder—our response to their reply. The deadline was late July 2021.

Unlike the Company, we would meet that deadline. Not because the tribunal deserved our compliance, given how they'd treated the Company's repeated delays, but because we weren't going to provide them with any excuse to rule against us on procedural grounds.

I worked with my team to craft every paragraph of the rejoinder. We addressed every new argument the Company had raised. We used their own documents to refute their claims. We highlighted the contradictions and inconsistencies.

And we stood on the settlement agreement. Valid. Voluntary. Evidenced by their own letter of appreciation. Binding.

We filed on July 30, 2021. On time. Complete. Properly executed.

* * * *

The pattern of tribunal behaviour had become undeniable. The Company got extensions without asking. They filed incomplete documents that were accepted. They missed deadlines without consequence. Mandatory rules were waived to accommodate them.

We got no extensions despite a pandemic lockdown. We were held to strict deadlines. Our objections were overruled.

I'd been documenting everything. Every deadline missed by the Company. Every extension granted. Every double standard. I had a timeline of the tribunal's actions that showed a clear pattern.

But I wasn't ready to challenge them yet. Not publicly. That would come later, when the pattern had become so apparent that even they couldn't deny it.

For now, I just kept notes. And kept working.

My eight-month analysis routine had given me what I needed: a complete understanding of the case. I knew their evidence better than they did. I'd found the contradictions in their documents. I'd identified the weaknesses in their claims.

But I still didn't have the theory. The elegant, simple argument that would tie everything together. The one insight that would make the tribunal—even a hostile tribunal—unable to rule against us.

I could feel it out there, just beyond my grasp. Something about the structure of the contract. Something about the timing of payments and deliveries. Something about what the Company was actually entitled to versus what they were claiming.

The pieces were all there. I just needed to see how they fit together.

That insight wouldn't come until much later—until I was deep into hearing preparation, when I understood that I needed something more than just good arguments. I needed a knockout punch.

But for now, as summer 2021 turned to fall, I was still searching for it. Still reading. Still analysing. Still trying to see the pattern that would unlock everything.

Chapter 4

The Pattern Emerges

The rejoinder we filed should have moved the case toward a hearing. In a typical arbitration, after the parties have exchanged their main submissions—claim, defence, reply, and rejoinder—the tribunal sets a schedule for the evidentiary phase. Witness statements are exchanged. Documents are finalised. Hearing dates are established.

But this was not a normal arbitration.

Throughout the proceedings, I watched as the pattern I'd first noticed during the pleadings phase continued and intensified. The Company would miss deadlines. The tribunal would grant extensions—sometimes without the Company even having to ask. We would meet our deadlines. The tribunal would hold us strictly to them.

I began keeping an even more detailed log. Not just notes anymore, but a comprehensive written record. Every procedural order. Every deadline. Every extension. Every double standard.

By early 2022, that log told a story that was impossible to ignore.

The Witness Statement Debacle

In September 2021, the tribunal ordered both parties to submit lists of witnesses who would testify at the hearing. The deadline was thirty days—October 20, 2021.

We submitted our list on time. It included government officials who could testify about the contract, payments made, and settlement negotiations. It also included top military personnel—though we knew from the Special Assistant that getting them to participate would be difficult.

The Company's list didn't arrive by the deadline. Or the week after. Or the week after that.

I wrote to the tribunal noting the missed deadline. The tribunal granted the Company more time. No explanation required from them. No justification needed. Just... more time.

* * * *

This happened again with the witness statements themselves. In November 2021, the tribunal ordered both parties to submit sworn statements from their witnesses by December 15, 2021.

We prepared ours carefully, had them signed and notarised, and filed them on schedule.

The Company submitted unsigned statements. Just drafts, basically. And they applied again, as previously, for permission to have them sworn at a later date—unspecified.

I objected. The Procedural Order No. 1 was clear. Witness statements should be sworn. That was the point—to ensure witnesses were attesting to the truth of their testimony under penalty of perjury.

The tribunal granted the Company's application. Their unsigned statements would be accepted as properly filed, with the option to have them sworn at some unspecified future date.

We had submitted sworn statements on time. They had submitted unsigned drafts late. And the tribunal treated both as equivalent.

I made a note in my log: *December 20, 2021 - Tribunal accepts unsigned witness statements from Claimant. In practical terms, the ruling created a precedent in which formal compliance with applicable rules was no longer required of the Claimant.*

The Question of Arbitration Costs

The issue of arbitration costs had become an ongoing administrative matter by early 2022.

The tribunal had set its fees at the outset—substantial amounts, as was normal for a case of this magnitude. Under the UNCITRAL Rules, if one party fails to pay its share of the costs, the other party must advance the full amount, or the tribunal may suspend or terminate the proceedings.

The Federal Government, my client, had decided not to contribute to the arbitration costs. The reasons were complex and political, but the effect was simple: the full financial burden fell on the Company.

I had informed the tribunal of the government's position earlier in the proceedings. The tribunal had taken note. The rules provided clear mechanisms for handling this situation—the Company could advance the full costs and seek reimbursement in the Award, or the tribunal could suspend proceedings until both parties paid their shares.

But as we moved toward the hearing, I could sense the tribunal's growing frustration with this issue. It came up in correspondence, in scheduling discussions, in the general tenor of the tribunal's communications. The government's decision not to pay was becoming a point of tension.

I expected that this matter would be addressed directly at the upcoming pre-hearing meeting in March. What I didn't expect was how the tribunal would choose to characterise it.

Team Morale

My team felt the weight of the pattern by this point. In our meetings throughout February and March 2022, the lawyers who'd been working alongside me for more than two years began expressing concerns.

"They're not even pretending to be neutral anymore," "The perception of neutrality had, by that point, become difficult to sustain," one said after the tribunal had denied yet another reasonable procedural application we'd made.

"Should we be documenting this?" another asked. "In case we need to... I don't know, challenge them somehow?"

"We're already documenting it," I said, gesturing to the thick file on my desk that contained my procedural log. "Every deadline, every extension, every ruling. We have the complete record."

"And what are we going to do with it?"

That was the question I'd been asking myself. The tribunal's conduct had gone beyond what I considered the normal range of discretionary rulings. It appeared to show consistent favouritism toward one party and hostility toward the other party.

But challenging arbitrators is serious. It's not something you do lightly. It requires grounds, evidence, careful consideration of timing and strategy. If you don't succeed, you've created an adversarial relationship with the people who will ultimately decide your case.

"For now, we keep doing our job," I said. "We file everything on time. We object when appropriate. We preserve the record. And we prepare the best defence possible. If it becomes necessary to challenge the tribunal formally, we'll have everything we need."

The lawyer who'd become closest to me during this case said quietly, "It's already necessary. The pattern is clear."

"Yes," I admitted. "It is. But we need something more than a pattern. We need a specific incident that crosses the line so obviously that even they can't deny it."

I didn't know then that such an incident was coming. That in less than two months, something would occur during a pre-hearing procedural meeting that would leave me no choice but to act.

Support from the Special Assistant

Throughout this period, I continued working with the Special Assistant. He remained my most reliable source of information and support from the government side. While other officials seemed content to let the case proceed without much involvement, the Special Assistant understood what was at stake and what was required for us to prevail.

He provided what documents he could access from the archives. He shared information about the Company's activities—their continued lobbying of government officials, their attempts to pressure the NSA and the AG for a settlement, and their public relations campaign painting themselves as victims of a government breach.

"They're working every angle," he told me during one of our meetings at his office in February 2022. "Legal, political, media. They're sophisticated operators."

"Have they approached anyone in government recently about settling?" I asked.

"They've tried. Letters to the National Security Adviser, requests for meetings, and intermediaries making inquiries. The Company's counsel even wrote to the Attorney General, urging him to settle—offering a specific amount and suggesting they had the upper hand in the arbitration, that our defence was weak."

I looked at him sharply. "They said our defence was weak?"

"The tone of the letter was confident. Almost dismissive. As if the outcome were already decided in their favour."

"So far, the NSA hasn't engaged. But the pressure is there."

"And if the tribunal rules in their favour?"

The Special Assistant's face darkened. "Then the pressure to pay will become enormous. Three billion dollars. Even if we challenge the , there will be voices saying we should pay and move on. Especially if the Company is offering to settle for less than the full amount."

"Which is exactly their strategy. File for three billion, make it painful, then offer to settle for one or two billion and look reasonable."

"Exactly. So, we need to win. Not just on technical grounds, but decisively. No ambiguity, no room for the Company to claim moral victory even in defeat."

I thought about our defence. It was strong. The settlement agreement was robust evidence. The Company's own documents supported our case. But I still felt like something was missing. The argument that would make victory not just probable, but compelling.

"We'll win," I said with more confidence than I felt. "The evidence is on our side."

"The evidence has been on our side from the beginning," the Special Assistant said quietly. "But the tribunal..."

He didn't finish the sentence. He didn't need to. We both knew what he meant.

The procedural environment had become openly hostile.

Moving Toward the Hearing

As winter 2022 turned to spring, the case moved into its final pre-hearing phase. The tribunal issued orders for the exchange of remaining evidence, interrogatories, and discoveries for the compilation of hearing bundles, as well as logistical arrangements.

And the pattern continued. The Company would file things late, incompletely, or not at all. The tribunal would accommodate them. We would file precisely on time, exactly as ordered. The tribunal would accept our submissions without comment—as if we were simply doing what was expected, while the Company was somehow deserving of special consideration.

The hearing was scheduled for August 2022. We were less than six months away from the moment when all the evidence would be presented, all the arguments made, all the procedural history would culminate in a final showdown.

My team was exhausted. Nearly three years of relentless work, of fighting not just the Company but also what appeared to be a pattern of decisions that consistently favoured them. To my team and I, it felt like we were up against the tribunal. But we were almost there.

"I know this has been difficult," I told them during one of our team meetings in early March. "I know the tribunal's conduct has been demoralising. But we're almost there. The hearing is our chance to present everything. To show them evidence they can't ignore, arguments they can't refute. We just need to hold on a little longer."

"Do you really think they'll rule fairly at the hearing?" one asked. "After everything we've seen?"

"I think when the evidence is presented in full, when we've made our case thoroughly and completely, the strength of our position will be undeniable," I said. "We're going to make it very difficult for them to rule against us."

I hoped that was true. I believed it had to be true because the alternative—that we could present overwhelming evidence and still lose was too unjust to contemplate. The alternative—that overwhelming evidence could be disregarded—would represent a failure of the arbitral process itself.

Scheduling the Pre-hearing Procedural Meeting

In early March, the tribunal scheduled a pre-hearing procedural meeting for March 17. The purpose was to finalise logistics, confirm hearing dates, and address any last-minute issues before the evidentiary hearing.

I prepared for the meeting carefully. There were procedural matters to discuss—timing of witness examinations, use of technology for the hearing, and arrangements for document presentation. Routine issues that needed to be resolved before we could proceed efficiently.

But I also prepared for something else. I'd been documenting the tribunal's conduct for more than eighteen months. I had a comprehensive record of procedural rulings that appeared to show a consistent pattern of indulging the Company. If that pattern continued during this meeting in a way that clearly justified a formal challenge, I would need to be ready to act.

I pulled out my procedural log and reviewed it. Page after page of entries. Deadlines missed by the Company with no consequences. Deadlines we met, enforced strictly. Applications granted to them, denied to us. Rules waived for their benefit, applied rigorously against us.

It was comprehensive. It was thoroughly documented. In my professional judgment, the record was damning. And if I needed to raise a formal challenge against the tribunal, it would provide the evidence.

But I hoped it wouldn't come to that. I hoped the meeting would be professional, neutral, and focused on logistics. I hoped I could get through the hearing without having to take the extraordinary step of challenging the arbitrators' impartiality.

That hope died on March 17, 2022.

The meeting was scheduled for the afternoon via ZOOM. All parties would participate remotely—the three arbitrators, the Company's counsel, my team, and I—just a procedural meeting to finalise details before the hearing.

Chapter 5

March 17, 2022

The ZOOM meeting opened with the familiar grid of video squares. The presiding arbitrator in his office, the two co-arbitrators in theirs, the Company's counsel, my team, and myself. Nine faces on a screen, about to have what should have been a routine procedural discussion. Nine participants for what the agenda described as a routine procedural conference on arbitration costs and hearing logistics.

The presiding arbitrator began. His voice came through clearly. "Good afternoon, everyone. Thank you for joining. Let's begin with an update on the status of arbitration fees and costs."

I had my notepad ready. I knew this topic would come up—it had been a recurring issue since the government decided not to contribute to the costs. But I expected a straightforward update: amounts paid, amounts outstanding, and a reminder that the Company would need to advance the full costs per the tribunal's previous orders, given the government's decision not to contribute.

What I got instead was something entirely different.

"As you know," the presiding arbitrator continued, "the Respondent has failed to contribute to the arbitration costs. This remains a significant concern for the tribunal."

Then he said something that made me stop writing mid-sentence.

Then he made a statement that, as I understood it, characterised the Federal Government's failure to pay arbitration fees as a breach of contract.

I looked up from my notepad, uncertain whether I'd heard correctly. But before I could fully process the implication, the Claimant-appointed arbitrator spoke, appearing to reiterate the same statement. His statement also seems to characterise the non-payment of fees as a breach of contract.

These statements of two arbitrators appeared to express a preliminary conclusion on the merits before the hearing had begun—a conclusion that the government I represented had breached the contract.

My co-counsel shot me a look off-camera. I could see the same alarm in his eyes that I felt.

What made this particularly jarring was something the Claimant had alleged in their submissions: that it was a notorious fact that the Federal Government of Nigeria breaches international agreements. And now, here were two members of the tribunal appearing to endorse that characterisation.

The case before us—the entire three-billion-dollar arbitration—was based on the Company's allegation that the government had breached the contract. That was the central dispute we were supposed to be resolving at the hearing. Had the government breached? Had the Company been wronged? Was the settlement agreement valid?

These were questions of fact and law to be determined after hearing evidence, after examining documents, and after considering arguments from both sides.

And here were two arbitrators, before the evidentiary hearing had even begun, making statements that seems to imply the government was in breach.

I carefully unmuted my microphone, choosing my words. "Sir, with respect, the question of whether there was a breach of contract is the central issue to be determined at the hearing. We have a settlement agreement that both parties voluntarily signed, resolving all outstanding issues. The question of breach—if any—is precisely what we're here to litigate."

I paused, then added, "The UNCITRAL Rules provide specific mechanisms for dealing with non-payment of costs. The tribunal can suspend proceedings, or the Claimant can advance the full costs and seek reimbursement in the . Those are the remedies contemplated by the rules."

The presiding arbitrators' expression didn't change. The implication hung in the air—that the failure to pay fees constituted a breach—that the government's failure to pay fees was, in the tribunal's view, a breach.

I made a contemporaneous note in my pad: *The presiding arbitrator appears to characterise FG's failure to pay fees as a breach of contract. Claimant-appointed arbitrator concurs. This is the central merits question to be decided after hearing evidence and legal arguments. If this is their position, both are prejudging the central issue before the hearing.*

The meeting continued, but the statements raised immediate concerns about the tribunal's impartiality. Two members of the tribunal may have revealed their view of the case before hearing a single piece of evidence.

The meeting moved on to other topics, but I was only half-listening now. My mind was racing. I was thinking about what had just happened.

This wasn't indulgence in the sense of favouring one party's procedural requests. This was, I believe, something far more serious. At the time, I understood the statement as expressing a conclusion on the merits before hearing evidence.

* * * *

The next topic—though it almost wasn't discussed at all—was the Company counsel's correspondence directly to the Attorney General.

Over the past few months, their lead lawyer had been writing to the AG's office without copying me—letters seeking settlement, requesting meetings, applying pressure outside the arbitration process. Giving the impression that they had the upper hand in the arbitration and that our defence was weak. Sounding confident, almost dismissive, as if the case had already been decided in his favour.

I'd raised this issue in a letter to the tribunal before the meeting, asking them to address this improper ex parte communication with my client.

But when the meeting began, the issue wasn't on the agenda.

The tribunal had simply... not scheduled it.

Once the discussion of the status of arbitration fees and costs was concluded, the government-appointed arbitrator spoke up. "Mr Chairman, I believe counsel for the Respondent raised a concern about letters from the Claimant's counsel to government officials. Perhaps we should address that?"

It was gracious of him to remind the presiding arbitrator. But telling that he'd needed to.

The presiding arbitrator nodded. "Ah, yes. Mr Oji, please state your concern."

I began explaining. The Company's counsel had been communicating directly with my client, bypassing me entirely. Under basic professional ethics and arbitration protocol, parties communicate through their counsel, not around them. These letters were—

The Company's counsel cut me off. "We were simply exploring settlement—"

I continued. "—improper and should not have—"

He interrupted again. "The circumstances required direct communication—"

"—been sent without copying opposing counsel," I finished, speaking over him.

The presiding arbitrator watched this exchange without intervention. No "Please let counsel finish." No "One at a time." He simply let the Company's counsel interrupt me repeatedly, trying to drown out my objection.

When I finally got my full statement out, the presiding arbitrator turned to the Company's counsel. "Can you explain these letters? Why were they sent directly to government officials rather than through opposing counsel?"

The Company's counsel responded smoothly. "We were attempting to explore settlement possibilities. Given the circumstances, we felt direct communication with decision-makers was appropriate."

"But you should copy opposing counsel," the presiding arbitrator said mildly. It was, at best, a gentle suggestion—not a rebuke, not a warning, just an observation.

His body language conveyed something else entirely. A slight nod. A permissive expression. The message was clear: he saw nothing seriously wrong with what the Company's counsel had done.

Then the Company's counsel shifted to his defence. "In any event, the Federal Government has made it impossible for us to proceed normally. They invaded our offices. They arrested our staff. They confiscated all our documents related to this case. We've been operating under extraordinary constraints."

I sat up straighter. This was new. The Company had previously made vague allegations of government harassment, but now their counsel was stating it as fact before the tribunal.

I unmuted. "Sir, I need to respond to that allegation. The Company's representatives were involved in activities that raised national security concerns—unrelated to this arbitration. If the Company were exposed to other legal jeopardy. If there were law enforcement actions, they were for legitimate reasons unrelated to this case. But more importantly, I would note that the Company has produced two cartons of documents for this arbitration. If their documents were confiscated, how did they produce all that evidence?"

"The confiscation happened after we'd already prepared our case," the Company's counsel shot back.

"Then that proves the confiscation, if it occurred, didn't impair your ability to participate in this arbitration," I said. "You had everything you needed."

I thought that was a strong response—a clear rebuttal. The logical inconsistency in the Company's position was obvious.

But what happened next shocked me.

The presiding arbitrator leaned forward on his video screen. "Well, if there's evidence of this—evidence that the government invaded the Company's offices and confiscated documents—that would be very serious. That would be relevant to our consideration."

He was defending the Company, not as an arbitrator hearing competing positions, but as an advocate suggesting how the Company should prove their allegation.

I opened my mouth to object, but he continued. "Do you have evidence of this invasion and confiscation? If you do, you should provide it. The tribunal would need to consider it carefully." The tribunal would later adjourn the meeting to enable the Company to produce evidence of the government agents' invasion of the Company's offices and confiscation of documents.

He was prompting them, telling them what to do. Suggesting they should find evidence to support an allegation they'd just made.

The Company's counsel seemed slightly surprised by this assistance. "We can... yes, we can attempt to gather evidence of the government's actions."

"Please do," the presiding arbitrator said. "This could be material to the case."

I was stunned. A neutral arbitrator, hearing an unsupported allegation from one party, would say something like: "If you're making that allegation, you'll need to prove it. Bring your evidence to the hearing."

They wouldn't prompt the party to find evidence. They wouldn't suggest that the allegation was serious and material before any evidence had been presented.

The presiding arbitrator's suggestion that the Company produce evidence appeared to move beyond case management into substantive guidance on how to prove their allegation. The presiding arbitrator may be seen to have stepped into the arena and taken on the role of the Company's advocate.

I made another contemporaneous note: *The presiding arbitrator suggested that the Company should produce evidence of the alleged government invasion/confiscation, characterising it as "very serious" and "relevant" before any evidence is presented.*

* * * *

The meeting continued for another hour. Other procedural issues were discussed—hearing logistics, document presentation technology, and witness scheduling. But I was barely present. My mind kept returning to what I'd witnessed.

Two arbitrators had appeared to characterise the government's non-payment of fees as a breach of contract—the central merits question—before the evidentiary hearing.

The presiding arbitrator suggested to the Company how it might prove an unsupported allegation, offering guidance that appeared to cross the line from case management into substantive assistance.

The pattern I'd been documenting had just escalated. This went beyond procedural decisions that consistently favoured one party. This appeared to be a pre-judgment of the merits—and active guidance to help that party prove their case.

When the meeting ended and everyone logged off, I sat in my office staring at my notes.

My senior lawyers came in immediately. "That was..."

"Unbelievable," I finished. "The statements made during the March 17 meeting raised concerns about whether the tribunal had pre-judged the case or formed preliminary views on the merits before hearing evidence."

"That was concerning," one said carefully.

I looked at my notes, then at the procedural log I had been maintaining for eighteen months. The file was thick now—dozens of documented instances in which the tribunal had granted the Company procedural flexibility while strictly enforcing deadlines against us, and consistently favoured one party's position.

And now this: statements that appeared to pre-judge the merits, and guidance that appeared to assist one party in building their case. The clearest basis, in my assessment, for serious doubts as to their impartiality.

"What do we do?"

"We challenge them," I said. "Formally. Under the UNCITRAL Rules. We request that the presiding arbitrator and the Claimant-appointed arbitrator recuse themselves from this case."

"That's a serious step," one of them said. "If we challenge them and they refuse to withdraw, we're going to have to continue with a tribunal we've openly challenged. That could make things worse."

"It can't get worse," I said. "The pattern of conduct had reached a point where a formal challenge was necessary. Based on everything we had seen, it felt as though the case had already been decided and that the tribunal had aligned itself with the Company's position. The only question now was whether we documented that concern formally or pretended we hadn't seen it."

"In that kind of hostile situation, how do we proceed? " "And if they refuse to withdraw?"

"Then we proceed with the hearing anyway. And we make our case so airtight, so unassailable, that they have no choice but to rule in our favour. Because if they rule against us after we've proven our case, it will be obvious to everyone what happened here."

The lawyer closest to me said quietly, "You realise what this means, don't you? Even if we win—especially if we win—this will not end well for you."

He didn't elaborate, and he didn't need to.

At the time, I understood his comment as a warning about professional consequences that often follow challenges to authority. What followed would later reinforce the perception that the costs of that challenge were real.

But what was the alternative? Say nothing? Proceed as if I hadn't heard what I'd heard? Pretend the tribunal was impartial when they'd demonstrated the opposite?

"I know," I said. "But I don't have a choice. I have a duty to my client. I have a duty to the process. And I have a duty to the truth. In my professional judgment, their conduct gave rise to justifiable doubts as to their independence and impartiality. And I'm going to say so."

* * * *

I knew the timeline was tight. Under the UNCITRAL Rules, I had fifteen days from becoming aware of circumstances giving rise to justifiable doubts about the arbitrators' impartiality to file a formal challenge. The March 17 meeting had certainly given rise to such circumstances.

A challenge to arbitrators requires specific grounds, detailed evidence, and careful legal argument. But I also needed proof—the recording of what had been said.

I wrote to the tribunal requesting an unedited copy of the March 17 meeting transcript.

Then I waited. The transcript would provide the documentary evidence I needed. But days passed, and it didn't arrive.

The clock was ticking. I had barely fifteen days under the applicable rules to file my challenge. If I waited for the transcript and it arrived too late, I might miss the deadline entirely. And missing that deadline would mean losing the right to challenge at all.

I made the decision: I would file based on my contemporaneous handwritten notes from the meeting and the pattern of procedural conduct I had documented over the past eighteen months.

I pulled out my notes from March 17. During the meeting, I had written down the key statements as I understood them:

"Arbitrators appeared to characterise non-payment of fees as a breach of contract."

"Reference made to the government's alleged history of breaching international agreements."

"The presiding arbitrator suggested or prompted that the Company should produce evidence of the alleged office invasion."

These statements, combined with the systematic pattern of preferential treatment documented in my log, provided clear grounds for the challenge.

I began drafting. The letter needed to be comprehensive—laying out not just what happened on March 17, but the entire context of favouritism that had preceded it.

The grounds emerged as I wrote:

First, the arbitrators appeared to have pre-judged the merits. They had characterised the government's conduct as a breach of contract before hearing any evidence on the central question the arbitration was convened to resolve.

Second, the tribunal had shown a pattern of procedural decisions consistently favouring the Company, resulting in systematic preferential treatment and indulgence of the Company: flexible deadlines for them, rigid enforcement against us; rules waived for them, strictly applied against us. The pattern, documented over eighteen months, was systematic.

Third, the presiding arbitrator had offered substantive guidance to the Company on how to prove an allegation, moving beyond case management into what appeared to be advocacy. He'd prompted them to find evidence,

I wrote the challenge as a formal legal document. Factual. Particularised. Evidenced. Professional. Citing the relevant UNCITRAL Rules and the legal standards for challenging arbitrators based on justifiable doubts about their independence and impartiality.

By March 31, I had it ready. The letter of challenge was fifteen pages, methodically documenting what had happened, providing specific examples, and explaining why these circumstances gave rise to justifiable doubts.

The conclusion was measured and straightforward: "The circumstances give rise to justifiable doubts as to the impartiality and independence of the presiding arbitrator and the Claimant-appointed arbitrator. We respectfully request that they recuse themselves from this arbitration."

I reviewed it one final time. This was the point of no return. Once I filed this challenge, the relationship with the tribunal—already hostile—would become openly adversarial. There would be no pretence of collegiality or of routine procedural cooperation. No possibility of smooth proceedings.

But there was no alternative consistent with my obligations. I had a duty to my client. I had a duty to the process. And I had a duty to the truth.

I signed the letter. Scanned it. Attached it to an email. Addressed it to all parties—the three arbitrators and the Company's counsel, as required by the rules.

My cursor hovered over the send button.

This was the right thing to do. The necessary thing. The only thing consistent with my obligations as a legal counsel in the arbitration.

I clicked send.

The challenge was filed on March 31, 2022.

Then I waited. For the tribunal's response. And for the transcript I had requested.

* * * *

The tribunal's ruling on my challenge arrived in late April together with the verbatim transcripts of virtual meeting of 17 March, 2022.

The ruling was brief. Dismissive. The grounds I had raised were without merit, they said. The statements at the March 17 meeting had been taken out of context or misunderstood. The tribunal had shown no bias. My challenge stemmed from mischaracterisations of their conduct. They would not be withdrawing.

The ruling concluded: "The challenged arbitrators have considered the grounds put forward and find them insufficient to warrant withdrawal. The arbitration will continue with the current tribunal."

I read it twice. I wasn't surprised—I'd expected this outcome. But seeing it in writing made it final. The tribunal I had formally challenged for lack of independence and impartiality would continue to hear the case. There would be no course correction, no reconsideration, no acknowledgement of the pattern I had documented.

I opened the transcript immediately, searching for the passages that had formed the basis of my challenge—the characterisation of non-payment as breach, the reference to the government's alleged history, the guidance to the Company on evidence production.

They weren't there. The specific statements, as I had noted them, were not reflected in the transcript.

I read through it again, more carefully. Perhaps I'd missed them. Maybe they were worded differently in the transcript than I remembered. Possibly, I had misunderstood the phrasing at the moment.

But no. The statements I thought I heard and noted—the words that had prompted my challenge—were not reflected in the transcript.

I sat back, staring at the document. I had written them down in real time during the meeting. I had discussed them with my colleagues immediately after the meeting ended.

The transcript did not reflect the statements as I had understood and recorded them during the meeting, creating a discrepancy between my contemporaneous notes and the official record that I could not resolve.

I requested the electronic ZOOM recording itself to understand the discrepancy.

When the recording arrived, I watched it carefully. The statements weren't there either.

This created a profound problem: I had clear contemporaneous notes and a clear recollection. But the official record reflected something different.

I investigated whether technical issues could explain the discrepancy. I learned that, as a technical matter, the host can edit ZOOM recordings, and that the platform does not provide a reliable method for independently verifying whether any such edits have occurred. Technical experts confirmed that there is no reliable way to determine whether a ZOOM recording has been altered.

This information underscored the limits of ZOOM as a recording platform for formal proceedings.

I have no evidence that any editing occurred in this case, and the tribunal expressly denied that it had.

On May 26, 2022, I wrote to the tribunal. I explained that after reviewing both the ZOOM recording and the transcript, I had found that critical statements from my contemporaneous notes were absent from both. I informed them I was consulting with ZOOM Video Communications, Inc. to understand what might have happened, and had learned that cloud recordings were susceptible to adjustment without a trace, making them unreliable for formal proceedings. I rejected the recording and transcript as the true record of the meeting. I requested that the tribunal use other, more reliable methods of recording for future meetings or hearings.

The tribunal responded that no editing had occurred and that the recording was accurate.

I didn't know what to make of this. Perhaps there had been a technical glitch—something lost in transmission or recording. The tribunal's response was clear. I had no way to prove otherwise. But the discrepancy between what I had heard, noted, and discussed with my colleagues and what appeared in the official record remained unexplained. I had my handwritten notes and my clear recollection. But absent clear evidence of wrongdoing, pressing the issue would only deepen the conflict without resolving it.

* * * *

Under the UNCITRAL Rules, I had the right to pursue the challenge further by requesting that the appointing authority—in this case, the Secretary-General of the Permanent Court of Arbitration—review the matter and decide whether to replace the arbitrators.

I considered it. For several days, I weighed the options.

Pursuing the challenge would delay the hearing—probably for months, possibly longer. And there was no guarantee of success. The bar for removing arbitrators is high. I would need to prove not just that they appeared partial, but that no reasonable person could have confidence in their impartiality. Without the recording to back up my account of March 17, it wouldn't be easy.

And what would we gain? Even if the Permanent Court of Arbitration agreed with me and replaced the arbitrators, we would start over (de novo) with a new tribunal. More delays. More costs. More uncertainty.

Or we could proceed to the hearing in August. With a tribunal we had lost confidence in, yes. But also, with a defence so strong, so thoroughly documented, that even a hostile tribunal would struggle to rule against us without exposing themselves.

But I knew what I had heard. And I had my handwritten notes from March 17 to prove it.

To avoid escalating the matter or scandalising anyone, I decided not to pursue the challenge any further. I documented my concerns in my file and took no further action regarding the transcript and the recording itself.

I called the Special Assistant.

"They rejected the challenge," I told him. "No surprise, but it's official now."

"What are you going to do? Will you take it to the Permanent Court of Arbitration?"

"I'm leaning against it. It would delay everything for months, and there's no guarantee we'd win. Even if we did, we'd just be starting over with new arbitrators."

"So, you'll proceed with the hearing?"

"Yes. We proceed to the August hearing and present the strongest possible case. We find every piece of evidence, make every argument, document everything so thoroughly that the outcome becomes clear regardless of any preliminary views. If they rule against us despite overwhelming evidence, the would be vulnerable to challenge. But I don't believe it will come to that."

The Special Assistant was quiet for a moment. "That's a risk." "You're confident in the evidence?"

"Everything about this case has been a risk. But I believe the evidence will carry the day. It has to."

"The settlement agreement is clear. The Company's own documents support our case. We have a strong defence. We need to present it comprehensively."

The Special Assistant was silent again for a moment. "All right. Proceed to the hearing."

* * * *

I called my team together a few days later.

"We're proceeding to the August hearing," I told them. "The tribunal rejected the challenge and declined to withdraw. Our focus now is preparation. We build the strongest possible defence. We find every piece of evidence. We anticipate every objection, every argument in opposition. We make our case unassailable."

One of the lawyers asked the question I knew was coming: "And if they rule against us anyway?"

"Then we'll challenge the Award. But I don't think it will come to that. We document everything. We build a record that speaks for itself and to build a case so airtight, so unassailable, no tribunal will ignore."

"Do you really believe that?"

"I have to believe it. Because the alternative—that we can do everything right and still lose—that's not something I'm willing to accept."

The team nodded. They were exhausted, I could see that. Nearly three years of relentless work, of fighting not just the Company's claims but also what appeared to be an uphill procedural battle and the tribunal's apparent lack of independence and impartiality. But we were close now. The hearing was four months away—four months to build the case that would end this.

"One more thing," I said. "The settlement agreement is clear—we know that. The Company's own documents support our position—we know that too. But I keep feeling like there's a larger pattern we haven't fully articulated yet. Something about how the Company structured this entire arrangement: I've been reviewing their contracts, their correspondence, the timeline of events. There's something there—a framework that, if we can articulate it clearly, would show this wasn't simply a contract dispute. It was something more structured than that. I still feel like we're missing something. The argument that makes victory inevitable, not just probable. The insight that pulls everything together."

"What do you mean?"

"I'm not sure yet. But there's a pattern in what the Company did—how they structured this entire operation. I've been looking at their contracts, their correspondence, and the timeline of events. There's something there. Something that, if we can articulate it clearly, would show this wasn't just a breach-of-contract dispute. It was something else entirely."

I didn't know then what that insight would be. But I knew I needed to find it. And I had four months.

The hearing was scheduled for August 1-9, 2022. It was now early May. Summer stretched ahead—time to prepare, to refine, to discover what I was still missing.

I returned to the documents. To the contracts. To the timeline. Looking for the piece that would complete the puzzle.

Looking for the eureka moment that I sensed was coming. The insight that would complete the picture.

Chapter 6

Witnesses Who Wouldn't Testify

May ended with a small administrative victory that only underscored the larger problems that loomed ahead.

The tribunal secretary had circulated the hearing bundle—thousands of pages of contracts, correspondence, payment records, witness statements, expert reports, purchase receipts, invoices, shipping documents, Air Waybills, etc.—all organised and indexed for use at the August hearing. My team and I began reviewing it immediately, cross-referencing every document against our case files.

On May 29, I noticed something troubling: the sworn witness statement of one of our key government witnesses was missing from the bundle. I wrote to the secretary immediately, pointing out the omission. To his credit, he acted quickly. He recalled the bundles from all parties, inserted the missing statement in its proper place, and redistributed the corrected versions.

Problem solved. Efficiently, professionally, without drama.

If only the government bureaucrats had resolved the larger problem of the availability of our witnesses

* * * *

By early June, with the hearing two months away, I faced a reality I'd been trying to avoid: several witnesses with critical firsthand knowledge—witnesses whose testimony could directly refute the Company's core allegations—had declined to testify.

Not just declined. Refused. Adamantly.

I never fully understood the reasons. These were government officials and military officers who had participated in the contract's execution, witnessed key events, and had direct knowledge that contradicted the Company's claims. They had provided me with information privately—detailed accounts of what had actually happened, documents supporting the government's position, and explanations of the operational timeline.

But testify publicly? On the record? At a hearing where they would face cross-examination from the Company's counsel?

No.

The most crucial was Brig. Gen. Umut Wang. According to the information I'd gathered, he had been the officer seconded by the Nigerian Army to serve as the liaison between the Office of the National Security Adviser, the Nigerian Army, and the Company during the operation. His assignment had included monitoring the arrival and deployment of Company military inventories—arms, ammunition, weapons systems, helicopters, combat vehicles, equipment, and personnel. He had been present for the entire operational phase.

More importantly, he had travelled to China with the Company's representative after the settlement agreement was signed to take charge of leftover military inventory on behalf of the government. That trip—its timing, its voluntary nature, its occurrence after the settlement—directly contradicted the Company's claim that their representative had been coerced into signing the agreement.

I constructed our defence precisely on the role of Brig. Gen. Wang had played. He was the only person who could provide direct evidence of the equipment the Company had actually deployed to Nigeria, when it arrived, and when operations commenced. These were the central factual disputes: the government maintained that the Company had failed to deploy the agreed inventory within the contractual timelines; the Company asserted it had performed exactly as contracted.

Brig. Gen. Wang could definitively resolve the factual dispute. His testimony, supported by deployment records and his contemporaneous observations, would prove whether we were right or wrong. The evidence existed. The witness existed. He had provided that information to me in our private discussions.

But he would not testify.

Then there was Gen. Hector Francis. According to the settlement agreement itself, he had signed as a witness for the government. That meant he had witnessed the signing—or at minimum, he had been present when the parties executed the agreement.

The Company's entire three-billion-dollar claim rested on one central allegation: that their representative had been coerced and intimidated by Col. Ashley into signing the settlement agreement. The Company's representative had made this claim in his witness statement. It had been corroborated by Mr James Black another Company witness who claimed to have observed the alleged coercion.

Col. Ashley had denied it categorically. He stated that the settlement had been negotiated, that the final agreement closely tracked the settlement framework the Company itself had proposed, and that he hadn't even been in the room when the agreement was signed.

Gen. Francis could resolve this dispute. As the government's witness to the signing, he was the most appropriate person to testify about the circumstances. Had there been coercion? Intimidation? Duress? He had been there. He knew.

The Company's witness was prepared to testify. Had submitted a witness statement. Would appear at the hearing to describe what he claimed to have seen.

Gen. Francis would not.

* * * *

I couldn't simply accept this. The stakes were too high. Three billion dollars. The government's credibility in international arbitration. The precedent it would set if false allegations could succeed through the absence of contradictory testimony.

So I tried everything within the formal channels available to me.

On June 20, I wrote directly to Gen. Francis, explaining why his testimony was crucial, enclosing a draft witness statement based on what he had previously told me, and requesting that he attend the August hearing. The letter was respectful, professional, and urgent.

I wrote to Brig. Gen. Wang, the same day, made the same case: the defence depended on what he knew, what he had witnessed, what he could testify to under oath.

I wrote to the National Security Adviser, explaining that these officers possessed the best evidence the government could present—direct testimony from participants who could disprove the Company's allegations. I requested his intervention to ensure they testified.

The NSA's office responded by telephone, but not with the answer I'd hoped for. They explained that the NSA couldn't compel serving military officers to testify. Only their direct superior—the Chief of Army Staff—had that authority. They directed me to contact the Chief of Army Staff.

On June 22, I wrote to the Attorney General of the Federation. As the government's chief legal officer, surely he could appreciate the evidentiary crisis we faced. I laid out the case: why these witnesses were essential, what they could testify to, and what would likely happen if they didn't appear.

The Attorney General did not reply.

On July 13, following the NSA office's guidance, I wrote to the Chief of Army Staff. I explained the situation, the witnesses' roles, the evidence they possessed, and the consequences of their absence. I requested that he direct them to submit witness statements and attend the hearing.

The Army Secretary responded. His letter was polite but firm: I had no standing to make such requests directly to the Chief of Army Staff. Only the Attorney General could make that request on behalf of the government.

I had come full circle. The NSA couldn't help—direct me to the Army. The Army couldn't help—I must go through the AG. The AG wouldn't respond.

Meanwhile, the hearing date approached. August 1. Then August 8 and 9 for witness testimony. Six weeks away. Five weeks. Four weeks.

* * * *

Somewhere in this period—I don't recall exactly when, but the information reached me through someone who would know—I learned that Brig. Gen. Wang had said he would resign his commission rather than testify.

I sat with that for a while.

A military officer, willing to end his career rather than provide testimony in a case where the government he served faced a three-billion-dollar claim based on allegations he knew—from his direct personal involvement—to be false.

I never understood it. I still don't.

Perhaps there were pressures I didn't know about. Perhaps there were concerns about repercussions I couldn't see. Perhaps there were reasons that made sense from his perspective but remained invisible to mine.

What I did understand was that we would go into the hearing without the witnesses who could most directly refute the Company's core factual allegations. Without the officer who had monitored the equipment deployment and could testify to the delays. Without the witness to the settlement signing, who could confirm there had been no coercion.

We would have Col. Ashley, who had been stalwart throughout. We would have the documentary evidence—contracts, payment records, correspondence, shipping manifests. We would have the settlement agreement itself.

But we wouldn't have the firsthand testimony.

* * * *

There was one success from this period of letters and requests.

In my letters to the NSA and the AG, I had noted my concerns about security at the hearing. The Company's conduct throughout the arbitration—the attempted witness tampering, the aggressive tactics, the veiled threats in correspondence—suggested they might resort to intimidation or worse if they felt the hearing wasn't going their way. The hearing was scheduled to take place in a private law office in Abuja, not a government facility with built-in security.

I had requested armed security for the hearing venue for the days when our witnesses would testify.

The NSA's office arranged it. Armed personnel would be present outside the premises. Our witnesses and counsel would have protection.

It was something. A practical measure. A precaution that might prove unnecessary, but provided reassurance nonetheless.

But it wasn't the intervention I'd actually needed. Security guards couldn't testify about the deployment timelines for equipment. Armed protection couldn't provide eyewitness accounts of the signing of the settlement agreement.

* * * *

By late July, I had accepted the reality. The witnesses who wouldn't speak simply wouldn't speak. No amount of letters, requests, or official interventions would change that.

We would have to win the case with the evidence and witnesses we had.

The settlement agreement was still valid and binding. The Company's own documents still contained contradictions we could exploit. Col.

Ashley's testimony, combined with the documentary record, still presented a strong defence.

But I knew—and my team knew—that we were going into the hearing without the best evidence the case permitted. We were fighting with one hand tied behind our backs.

And then, in the final week of July, everything changed.

Not because a witness changed his mind. Not because a General decided to testify after all.

But because on a Friday morning, standing in my bathroom with soap still on my hands, I recognised something in the contract's structure I'd read a hundred times before.

Something that made the missing witnesses less critical than I'd thought.

Something that would change everything.

Chapter 7

Eureka

It was a Friday morning in late July—an ordinary workday. I was in my bathroom getting ready for the office, going through the routine I'd followed thousands of times—shower, shave, dress for another day of managing cases and clients and the endless demands of running a law firm.

But my mind wasn't on the routine. It was on the case. The three-billion-dollar arbitration that had consumed three years of my life. The hearing was less than two weeks away. We were as prepared as we could be. Strong arguments. Solid evidence. The settlement agreement that should end the case.

But against a tribunal whose procedural decisions had consistently concerned me? Was it enough?

Where I describe procedural decisions or conduct in this chapter, I do so from the perspective of counsel directly involved, based on the record and circumstances as they appeared to me at the time.

The soap was still on my hands when the thought arrived.

Not gradually, not through careful analysis, but all at once—complete, devastating, undeniable.

The contract was staged.

I stood there, water running, and felt everything click into place.

The contract between the government and the Company wasn't a simple purchase agreement. It was organised in stages. Stage one: procurement of equipment within one month. Stage two: recruitment and personnel training. Stage three and beyond: actual operations.

Each stage had specific deliverables. Specific timelines. Payment tied to performance.

And the contract had been terminated—by mutual agreement, documented in the settlement—before the later stages had been performed.

If the contract was staged and terminated before those stages were completed, the Company couldn't claim payment for work that was never performed. They could claim damages for breach of contract—if they could prove it. But they hadn't claimed breach of contract. They couldn't claim lease rental fees for equipment that hadn't been delivered before termination. They couldn't claim for stages that never happened.

It was that simple. That elegant. That, if accepted, undermined the legal foundation of their three-billion-dollar claim.

* * * *

I didn't know it then, standing there with soap still on my hands, but twenty-five months after the hearing ended, the tribunal would adopt this exact analysis.

They would call the contract "STAGED"—their word, in capital letters, as if it were obvious. "Multiple phases contingent on delivery and performance," they'd write.

They would accept the compartmentalisation I was frantically working out in my head—Category A, Category B, Category C, D, E. They'd agree that payment for each stage depended on completion of the prior stage.

They would find that the Company had failed to perform Stage 1—failed to deliver equipment on time and committed a "continuing breach" of fundamental contract terms.

And they would conclude exactly what I was realising at that moment: "If it fails to perform its supply obligation in Category A, it will not be entitled to payment in Category B."

The Company's three-billion-dollar claim was mathematically impossible.

I knew it was compelling. I knew it was unanswerable—unassailable. But I didn't know the tribunal would react to it. I just knew I'd found something. Something that felt true in a way that transcended hope or strategy.

The kind of insight that changes everything.

* * * *

I ran. Didn't rinse the soap off. Didn't dry my hands. Just straight to my study, water dripping on the floor, my mind already racing ahead to the implications.

I grabbed a legal pad and started writing. Fast, almost frantically, trying to capture the thought before it slipped away.

Contract = staged performance
Stage 1: Equipment procurement (1 month)
Payment: Full funding provided

Performance: Failed to deliver on time

Stage 2: Personnel
Stage 3+: Operations

Contract terminated before later stages performed
Settlement agreement = mutual termination

Company's claim = Payment for unperformed stages
= Lease fees for equipment never delivered
= Compensation for work never done

Legal theory: No entitlement to payment for unperformed contract stages

I kept writing, the argument developing as I went. This wasn't just about the settlement agreement anymore. This was about the fundamental structure of the contract. About what the Company had been paid for versus what they'd delivered. About what they were entitled to versus what they were claiming.

The settlement agreement remained crucial—it proved that both parties had agreed to end the contract. But now I had something more. A theory that explained why the Company's claims were baseless, even if you looked past the settlement.

They were claiming three billion dollars for stages of a contract that had never been performed. For equipment that had never been delivered. For lease fees on equipment that hadn't arrived before termination. For work that had never been done.

And I could prove all of it using their own documents. The shipping records showing late delivery. The payment records showing they'd been paid in full. The contract itself showing the staged structure. The settlement showing mutual termination.

I wrote for almost two hours, filling page after page with notes, arguments, and supporting points. By the time I finally stopped, I had the complete theory laid out. The argument that would make the outcome clear. The argument that would present the tribunal with undeniable evidence. The argument that would leave little room for a lawful decision in the Company's favour.

I looked at what I'd written and felt something I hadn't felt in months: certainty.

This was it. The knockout punch I'd been searching for.

Nearly every case has a knockout punch. Trial law experience has taught me that. If you seek hard enough, you will find it.

* * * *

I got to the office late and called my team. Told them to come to my office immediately. By ten a.m., all three of my senior lawyers were sitting around my conference table, looking at me with curiosity and concern.

"I have it," I said. "The argument that wins this case."

I walked them through it—the staged contract. The termination occurring before the later stages began. The Company's claim for payment on unperformed work. The legal theory that made it all unassailable.

They listened, asked questions, pushed back on weak points, and helped me refine and strengthen the argument.

"This is extraordinary," one of them finally said. "This doesn't just supplement our case. This is our case. Everything else supports this central theory."

* * * *

What I couldn't tell them—what I wouldn't know for twenty-five months—was that the tribunal would adopt this framework word-for-word.

They would use our compartmentalisation structure. They would quote our interpretation of payment milestones. They would agree that the contract required delivery before the second stage payment.

One hundred eighty-seven pages of post-hearing brief. The tribunal would read every word. We'd know because they used our exact framework in their ruling.

But that was twenty-five months away. At that moment, in my office, it was just an argument. A theory. A hope that we'd found the truth.

* * * *

"Exactly," I said. "The settlement agreement proves they agreed to terminate. But this explains why their current claims are legally baseless, even if you ignore the settlement. They're claiming money for contract stages that never happened."

The lawyer who'd become closest to me during this case asked the critical question: "When do we deploy this?"

I'd been thinking about that. "Not at the hearing."

They all looked surprised.

"Why not?" one asked. "This is our strongest argument. Why wouldn't we lead with it?"

"Because the hearing is two weeks away. If we present this at the hearing, the Company will hear it. They'll have time to adjust their strategy, to try to counter it, to find arguments against it. And given the pattern we've observed, they may receive assistance in doing so."

I let that sink in.

"There's another reason," I continued. "Over three years, I've watched how the tribunal treats arguments from each side. The Company can make broad assertions without evidence, and the tribunal engages seriously. We present documented proof, and they move on without comment. The Company's counsel argues positions unsupported by the contract, and the tribunal explores the implications. We cite binding legal authority, and they redirect the conversation."

One of my lawyers nodded slowly. "You think they'll discount it if we present it orally."

"I think they've shown a pattern of treating the Company's narrative as more credible than our evidence, regardless of what the record actually shows. That pattern has held for three years—through every procedural battle, every evidentiary dispute, every deadline. I don't expect it to change at the hearing."

"So a written brief—"

"A written brief can't be interrupted mid-argument," I said. "It can't be minimised in the moment or reframed to mean something else. It has to be read in full, considered in its entirety. And if they dismiss it, that dismissal has to be explained in the Award—on the permanent record."

"But if we hold it until the post-hearing brief," I continued, "the hearing will be closed. The Company will have made their case. We'll have made ours. The tribunal will have heard all the evidence. And then, when they think they know everything that's been argued, we present this. In writing. Fully developed. Unassailable."

"By the time they realise what we've done, it's too late," the closest lawyer said, understanding. "They can't adjust. The Company can't respond effectively. The hearing is closed."

"Exactly. We present our other strong arguments at the hearing—the settlement agreement, the Company's own documents, all of it. We make a good case. But we save this for the post-hearing brief. The final argument, when they can't respond to it."

"That's risky," one of them said. "What if the tribunal rules against us based on what we present at the hearing?"

"They won't," I said. "The tribunal can't rule until parties submit the scheduled post-hearing briefs." "Because what we present at the hearing will be strong enough to create a solid foundation. We'll have the settlement agreement. We'll have the Company's contradictions. We'll have enough to make our case compelling. But then, in the post-hearing brief, we give them this. And suddenly ruling against us isn't just questionable—it's impossible. Because this argument, with the evidence we have, makes it so clear that ruling for the Company would require disregarding the plain terms of the contract and the documentary record."

* * * *

The strategy was sound. But it carried a risk I couldn't fully articulate.

If the tribunal had already decided—if they'd truly pre-judged the case before hearing our defence—then even the strongest post-hearing argument might not matter. They might simply ignore it. Rule against us anyway. Write an Award that disregarded the contractual structure we'd identified.

But if we were right—if the staged contract analysis were as clear as I believed—then the tribunal would have to address it. Would have to explain why they were ruling in favour of the Company despite the contract's explicit structure. Would have to justify three billion dollars for stages never performed.

And if they couldn't justify it, if they couldn't explain away the documentary evidence and the plain contractual terms, then maybe—just maybe—the post-hearing brief would give them a way out. A path to ruling in our favour that didn't require acknowledging they'd been wrong all along.

The tribunal could accept our analysis. Adopt our framework. Find the Company had failed to perform. Complete victory.

And never once mentioned that they'd seemed to favour the Company throughout the proceedings. Never acknowledge the procedural irregularities. Never address the concerning patterns we'd documented.

They could vindicate our case on the merits while erasing everything else from the official record.

I didn't realise then that this was exactly what would happen.

* * * *

We spent the rest of that day celebrating and refining. We went to a fancy restaurant that evening, the four of us, and over dinner and champagne, we worked through every angle of the argument. Testing it, strengthening it, making it bulletproof.

By the time we left that restaurant, I knew we had something special. Not just a good argument or a strong case. We had the argument, so well supported by documentary evidence, that it would be very difficult to rule against us.

Because the alternative—ruling against us despite this evidence—would require disregarding the plain contractual terms, the undisputed documentary record and basic principles of contract law.

* * * *

The hearing was still ahead. I would present our other arguments there—strong arguments, compelling evidence. I would cross-examine their witnesses. I would introduce our documents. I would do everything a lawyer does at an arbitration hearing.

But I would save this insight for after, for the post-hearing brief, when the Company couldn't respond, when the Company couldn't respond effectively to this new analytical framework.

For the moment when the outcome would become clear.

* * * *

In early June—weeks before my bathroom breakthrough—I received a phone call that would add another dimension to our case.

"Mr Oji, this is Colonel Ashley." The voice on the line was formal, military-precise. "I was one of the personnel involved in the operations with [the Company]. I understand the hearing is coming in August."

"Yes, Colonel. How can I help you?"

"I need to speak with you about something that happened before the arbitration began. Something the Company tried to do to me."

We arranged to meet at my office the following day. The Colonel arrived in civilian clothes, but his bearing—straight-backed, alert, disciplined—marked him as military even without the uniform.

He sat across from my desk and told me a story that confirmed my worst suspicions about the Company's tactics and raised serious concerns about the Company's conduct.

"Before the tribunal was even constituted," he said, "I was approached by a representative of the Company. He knew I'd been involved in the operations. He knew I'd be a potentially important witness if this matter went to arbitration."

"What did he want?"

"He wanted me to testify against the government. He offered me a substantial sum in millions of U.S. dollars. The plan was simple: I would retire from military service, testify that the government had breached the contract and wronged the Company, the Company would win the arbitration, and I would receive additional payments afterwards."

I sat forward. "How much money are we talking about?"

"Enough to retire comfortably. Enough to start a new life. He was very clear about what was on offer."

"And what did you tell him?"

The Colonel's expression hardened. "I told him no. I chose honour. I'm a serving officer. I took an oath. I'm not going to lie in a tribunal for money, no matter how much they offer."

"Did he try again?"

"Several times. Through different intermediaries. The offers kept coming. He sent me a draft witness statement for my signature. But my answer remained the same."

"Why are you telling me this now?"

"Because I want you to know what you're up against. This Company isn't just fighting a legal case. They're trying to corrupt the process. They're trying to buy witnesses, intimidate officials, and pressure the government through every channel they can find. And I thought you should know that before you go into that hearing."

After the Colonel left, I sat in my office thinking about what he'd told me.

What he described, if accurate, raised serious concerns about potential witness interference and attempts to influence the evidentiary process improperly.

This was highly sensitive information with potentially serious implications. If true, it would be evidence of serious misconduct—corruption of the arbitral process —proof of their comprehensive strategy to win by any means necessary.

If substantiated, this was information the tribunal would need to assess credibility and procedural integrity.

* * * *

Shortly after my meeting with the Colonel, the tribunal issued an order for something it called "pre-hearing briefs." I'd never encountered this term before—it wasn't in the UNCITRAL Rules, and the tribunal hadn't defined what exactly they wanted.

I objected immediately. I wrote to the tribunal explaining that there was no provision for pre-hearing briefs in the UNCITRAL Rules. The parties had already exhausted themselves on the facts through two complete rounds of written submissions—the Company's statement of claim and reply, our statement of defence and rejoinder. What purpose would another round of briefs serve?

More importantly, the pattern suggested a purpose behind this unusual order. It appeared designed to give the Company yet another opportunity to submit materials before the hearing. Another accommodation in the long pattern of favourable treatment I'd been documenting for three years.

I'd lost confidence in the tribunal.

The tribunal overruled my objection as they had overruled nearly every objection, application, or proposal I'd made throughout this arbitration.

The pre-hearing briefs would be required. Both parties would submit them simultaneously by July 16, 2022.

Fine, I thought. If they wanted a pre-hearing brief, I'd give it to them. And I'd use it strategically.

I spent several days in June preparing the brief. It laid out our key arguments: the settlement agreement was valid and binding; the Company had failed to perform as contracted; and their current claims were baseless attempts to undo a resolution they'd freely agreed to.

But I also included a section on the Company's conduct during the arbitration. Their delays. Their incomplete submissions. Their communications with government officials outside the arbitral process.

And most importantly, the alleged attempted bribery of Colonel Ashley.

I included the Colonel's sworn statement detailing the approach he'd received, the offers made, and his refusal. I annexed a copy of the draft witness statement that the Company's representative had allegedly provided to him for his deposition in support of their claim. If true, this would be evidence of attempts to corrupt the arbitral process.

The tribunal had specified that pre-hearing briefs should be submitted simultaneously—meaning both parties would file on the same day. At the same time, neither seeing the other's brief beforehand.

I emailed my pre-hearing brief to the presiding arbitrator—the soft copy to meet the deadline. I followed up by sending the original hard copy by courier for the official record, along with bound supporting exhibits, including the Colonel's sworn statement. Both submissions contained identical content.

Then I waited to see when the tribunal would circulate both briefs to all parties.

* * * *

It was during this period—in the final week of July, after the pre-hearing briefs should have been circulated—that I had my bathroom breakthrough. The eureka moment that would change everything.

But I'm getting ahead of myself. Let me return to the sequence of events.

As July progressed, we received the hearing bundle—a compilation of all documents to be used at the hearing. The tribunal secretary sent it electronically first, and then the hard copies: thousands of pages of contracts, correspondence, payment records, witness statements, expert reports.

My team and I began reviewing it immediately. We needed to know where every document was located, how to reference it quickly during the hearing, and which exhibits supported which arguments.

I was going through the table of contents when I noticed something odd.

My pre-hearing brief wasn't included.

I checked again, thinking I'd missed it. But no—neither brief was included in the bundle. I later learned that the Company hadn't submitted a pre-hearing brief at all. Only I had submitted one, and the tribunal had excluded it from the hearing bundle. After all the fuss about it. After overruling my application against it.

I checked the email I'd sent on July 16. It had gone to the presiding arbitrator's email address. I checked the courier confirmation for the hard copy. It had been delivered and signed for.

But my brief—including the evidence of alleged attempted witness tampering—wasn't in the hearing bundle.

I could have written to the tribunal demanding an explanation. I could have insisted they include it. But I'd spent three years watching this tribunal ignore my reasonable requests, overrule my proper objections, and accommodate every irregularity from the Company.

I wasn't going to waste the final days before the hearing fighting over this. The tribunal had received my brief. They knew what was in it. If they chose to exclude this evidence from the record, that was their decision—and it would be documented as part of the pattern I had been recording.

I needed to focus my energy on presenting our case at the hearing itself.

The hearing was now less than two weeks away. The tribunal had compiled a hearing bundle that excluded my pre-hearing brief—the only pre-hearing brief that had actually been submitted. The brief containing evidence of the Company's alleged attempt to corrupt a witness had not been included in the bundle.

I discussed it with my team. "This is concerning," I said. "They received the brief. But they're excluding it from the bundle."

"Why would they do that?" one lawyer asked.

"Maybe because it contains evidence the tribunal chose not to include in the hearing bundle. Evidence of the Company's attempts to suborn our witness and corrupt the process. Evidence that would be relevant to assessing their credibility and the integrity of their claims. Evidence that supports our argument that this arbitration, as conducted, raised serious questions about procedural balance and evidentiary fairness."

The lawyer closest to me said quietly, " The exclusion of this material was concerning—evidence that could have been material. The pattern suggested preferential treatment. It fits the pattern we've been documenting."

"Yes," I agreed. "That's exactly what they're doing."

This appeared to be more than a procedural irregularity. The tribunal was excluding relevant, material evidence from the hearing bundle without explanation. The exclusion had the practical effect of keeping potentially relevant material out of the hearing bundle, without explanation.

I made another note in my procedural log: *July 2022 - Tribunal excludes Respondent's pre-hearing brief from hearing bundle. The brief contained evidence of the Company's alleged witness tampering—no explanation for exclusion.*

* * * *

There were other issues in the final weeks before the hearing. Small things that, individually, might seem insignificant, but cumulatively demonstrated the tribunal's hostility and created additional challenges for our preparation.

We submitted a request for the detailed address of the hearing venue. The presiding arbitrator responded that this was the secretary's job, not his. Petty, but revealing.

We requested guidance on the timing of witness examinations—how long each witness would have, how breaks would be scheduled, and the logistics to plan. The presiding arbitrator said it would be handled at the hearing: no advance planning, no certainty, no ability to prepare our witnesses for what to expect.

Just another small obstacle, but revealing of the tribunal's disposition.

They were providing us with no assistance, no cooperation, and no advance certainty about how the hearing would be conducted.

My team's morale was low, but I was confident now in a way I hadn't been before. We had the eureka argument. We had our strategy. We knew how we would present our case.

"Can we actually win this?" one of them asked me during a preparation session.

I thought about the question carefully before answering. "On the merits? Absolutely. The evidence is overwhelming. The settlement agreement is unassailable. Their own documents prove they didn't perform. And now we have the staged contract argument that makes it all come together."

"But we're concerned about the pattern we've observed."

"I know," I said. "But we have something very difficult to disregard. We have an argument so strong, so clear, so supported by the evidence, that ruling against us would require ignoring the plain contractual terms and the documentary record. We're going to present them with evidence they cannot reasonably dismiss."

* * * *

We flew to Abuja the day before the hearing was scheduled to begin—myself, my three senior lawyers, and two support staff. We were staying at a hotel near the hearing venue, ready for the long days ahead.

That evening, while my team rested in their rooms, I stayed up late in mine, surrounded by files and documents and three years of accumulated knowledge about this case.

I thought about everything we'd been through. The Company's eighteen-month delay in filing its case. The tribunal's systematic indulgence of the Company. The challenge we'd filed and lost. The excluded pre-hearing brief and evidence. The hostile procedural rulings.

And I thought about what we were fighting for. Three billion dollars. But more than that, principle. Truth. The rule of law. The idea that evidence matters, that proper procedure matters, and that settlements freely made should be honoured.

I thought about the Special Assistant, still supporting us despite everything. About the Colonel who'd chosen honour over money. About my team, exhausted but still committed.

And I thought about the Company. Their claims, which we believed were without merit. The allegations of witness tampering. The aggressive litigation tactics. Their confidence that they could prevail through volume, influence and persistence.

We were ready—more than ready. We had prepared as well as anyone could. We knew the case inside and out.

And we had the argument that could make the outcome clear—waiting in reserve for the right moment to deploy it.

I looked at the contract one more time. The staged structure. The specific deliverables. The termination before the later stages could begin—stages that were never performed.

It was all there. Clear. Undeniable. Fatal to their claim.

Tomorrow, the hearing would begin. We would present our case. We would show the tribunal evidence that demanded serious consideration. We would cross-examine their witnesses and introduce our documents.

And then, after it was all over, after the hearing had closed and they thought they knew everything that had been argued, we would present the final argument.

The staged contract argument. The legal theory that made their three-billion-dollar claim not just wrong, but impossible.

* * * *

The tribunal would eventually agree with every word of that analysis.

They would find the contract was staged. That time was fundamental. That the Company had failed to deliver equipment within contractually stipulated deadlines. That payment for each stage depended on completion of the prior stage. That the Company was not entitled to compensation for stages never performed.

They would dismiss the Company's entire claim. All three billion dollars. And Award them nothing.

They would adopt our legal framework so completely that reading the Award would feel like reading our own brief reflected back at us.

But they would take twenty-five months to write it. Twenty-five months after a hearing where they'd announced they already had "a position" and had "formed their impression." Twenty-five months to adopt the analysis we'd present in our post-hearing brief.

And in those ninety-one pages, they would never explain the delay. Never address why an argument they found so compelling took over two years to accept. Never reconcile their pre-judgment statements with their ultimate agreement with our case.

The record would show pre-judgment. The Award would show vindication. And the gap between them would simply disappear.

* * * *

I went to bed that night confident.

Not hopeful. Not optimistic. Confident.

Because I knew something the tribunal didn't know yet. Something the Company didn't know.

I knew we had arguments that could not be reasonably ignored.

And I believed we would prevail.

Chapter 8

The Hearing

This chapter recounts events as they occurred during the hearing and reflects my contemporaneous observations and professional assessment as counsel for one of the parties.

The hearing venue was a purpose-built arbitration hearing room in Abuja—neutral ground, neither the tribunal's offices nor ours, just a rented space for nine days that would determine three billion dollars and three years of work.

We arrived early on August 1, 2022: my three senior lawyers, the two support staff, and I. We set up our materials at one long table—audio recording equipment, laptops, files, hearing bundles, and legal pads.

The three arbitrators sat at the head of the room. The presiding arbitrator in the centre, the two co-arbitrators flanking him. All three Senior Advocates of Nigeria. Two of whom I'd formally challenged for lack of independence and impartiality. All three men who'd rejected that challenge and made clear they intended to proceed unchanged.

The Company's counsel and his team arrived late. They sat opposite us in the room and set up their materials, just as we did.

The presiding arbitrator called the hearing to order at 10 a.m. "Good morning, everyone. We'll begin with preliminary matters before the Claimant presents its case."

I was taking notes, waiting for the routine opening statements, when the Company's counsel stood and made an announcement that changed everything.

"Mr Chairman, before we begin, I need to inform the tribunal and opposing counsel that we have amended the witness statement of Mr Doe. This is the sworn substitution of his earlier unsworn depositions."

I looked up sharply. Amended witness statements? At the hearing? After we'd received the hearing bundle, prepared our cross-examinations, and finalised our strategy?

The Company's counsel continued. "I should note that Mr Doe's statement contains two new paragraphs addressing additional matters that came to our attention."

Two new paragraphs. At the hearing. Without advance notice.

I stood immediately. "Sir, I object. We received witness statements months ago. We've prepared this hearing and our cross-examinations based on those statements. The Company cannot simply introduce new evidence at the hearing without allowing us to respond."

The Company's counsel responded smoothly. "These are sworn versions of statements that were previously unsworn. The tribunal had already accepted the unsworn versions. We're simply providing the formalised versions."

"With new content," I said. "Mr Doe's statement allegedly contains two new paragraphs. That's not a formality—that's new evidence introduced at the last possible moment."

The presiding arbitrator looked at the Company's counsel. "When did you prepare these amended statements?"

"Recently, sir. The new paragraphs in Mr Doe's statement address matters that we believe are relevant to the tribunal's determination."

I objected again. "Sir, the purpose of exchanging witness statements in advance is to avoid precisely this kind of surprise. If the Company has new evidence, it should have disclosed it with adequate time for the Respondent to prepare a response. Introducing it at the hearing prejudices our ability to respond effectively."

The presiding arbitrator considered this briefly. Then he said, "We'll allow the amended statements. However, we'll reserve the Respondent's right to respond. If you wish to submit rebuttal evidence after reviewing Mr Doe's testimony, you may do so. The Claimant will bear the costs of any late submission."

The Company's counsel nodded. "We accept that condition, sir."

I sat down and made a note: *Day 1 - Company introduces new witness statement at the hearing. Tribunal allows over objection. Reserved the right to respond.*

This was not how hearings were supposed to work. Witness statements were exchanged in advance precisely to avoid ambush. But the tribunal had just permitted exactly that—new evidence at the hearing, without advance notice, with only a vague promise that I could "respond later."

I looked at my team. They understood what had just happened. Another accommodation for the Company. Another departure from standard practice by a tribunal whose pattern of decisions we had been documenting for three years.

But we proceeded because we had no choice.

* * * *

The Company's case took three days—August 1, 2 and 3. They called their witnesses, presented their evidence, and made their arguments. It was comprehensive, professional, and well-organised.

But it was too simplistic without depth.

It was constructed on what we believed was a fundamental misunderstanding of the contract, the law, the facts and their own evidence.

Their theory was comprehensive and straightforward: the contract was a lease arrangement. They had procured military equipment—helicopters, armoured vehicles, weapons, ammunition—and leased it to the Nigerian government for the operation. The equipment belonged to them; Nigeria was merely renting it for the operation.

They had recruited and deployed foreign military personnel. They had conducted combat operations against Boko Haram in the North East of Nigeria, fully performing the contract. The government had terminated the contract improperly, pressured them into accepting a fraction of what they were owed, coerced them into signing a settlement agreement and forced them out of the country.

They argued that the government had then confiscated their equipment—the helicopters, vehicles, weapons—without compensation.

Therefore, they claimed, the government owed them the full contract value for services rendered, the monetary value of the confiscated equipment, lease rental fees for the six-month contract duration, cost overruns, damages for wrongful termination, and interest compounding from the inception of each obligation until full payment.

Three billion dollars.

I took notes as they presented. Listened to testimony—cross-examined witnesses. But I was also watching the tribunal.

And what I observed confirmed everything I'd believed about their lack of impartiality and was consistent with the pattern I had been documenting.

During Mr James Black's (one of the Company's witnesses) testimony, the presiding arbitrator asked questions that appeared to help clarify the Company's case. He prompted. He suggested. He gave the witness opportunities to expand on points that supported the Company's theory.

When Mr George Sweeny, the Company's principal, took the stand, he testified about the equipment allegedly provided. That the Company had performed its obligations fully. The presiding arbitrator nodded along, taking notes and asking follow-up questions that allowed the witness to elaborate.

But Sweeny's testimony contradicted his own company's documents.

The documents told a different story.

The contract, signed November 17, 2014, required:

- Helicopters within 21 days
- Vehicles within 14 days
- Weapons and ammunition within 21 days

The Company's own exhibits showed:

- Helicopter airway bill: January 30, 2015
- Vehicle airway bill: February 12, 2015
- Ammunition deliveries: throughout 2015, some as late as October

Not one item delivered within the contracted timeline. The Company's own documents proved it.

The tribunal would later create a detailed table of every delivery document the Company submitted. Forty items. Each with a date showing when the shipping process began—not when equipment arrived, not when it was deployed, but when someone initiated transport.

Not one item met the contract deadlines. The tribunal's own table, drawn from the Company's own evidence, would prove it.

What wasn't in the record was just as revealing as what was.

The Company had invoices. Airway bills. Packing lists. All showing the initiation of shipments—documents proving they'd sent something, somewhere.

But no arrival confirmations. No delivery receipts showing equipment had actually reached the battlefield. No signatures from receiving officers. No timestamps from Nigerian Customs showing when these shipments cleared. No Customs clearing documents.

During cross-examination, I asked about bank statements for local purchases. The Company's counsel objected. The presiding arbitrator sustained the objection.

Bank statements would have shown when the Company actually paid for supplies they claimed to have delivered on time. Wire transfer records would have revealed the timing of their payments to subcontractors. Financial documentation would have proved—or disproved—their timeline claims.

They never produced any of it.

The tribunal would later note this in their Award. When one party requests bank statements and the other refuses to produce them, "withholding evidence in law," the tribunal would write, is "fatal to the Claimant's case."

But that was twenty-five months away. At the hearing, the tribunal simply sustained the objection and moved on.

* * * *

But at the hearing, the presiding arbitrator simply nodded and said: "We have a full picture."

And then, during my cross-examination of Sweeny, something highly unusual happened.

The presiding arbitrator interrupted: "Quite honestly, we have a full picture of what may have happened. So why don't we limit it to what may need explanation from his cross-examination? Quite honestly, most of what you are asking up to now, of course, we sat here, and we have our position as we listen."

I stopped writing. Looked up from my notes.

We have a full picture. We have our position.

This was during the presentation of the Company's case, before we presented our defence. Before our witnesses had testified. Before we introduced our evidence. Before we presented our legal argument.

And the tribunal already had "a full picture" and "a position."

I looked at my team. They'd heard it too. One of them was writing furiously, capturing the exact words for the record.

We continued the cross-examination because we had no choice.

* * * *

The court reporter would capture every word. And it was in the verbatim transcript.

"We have a full picture." "We have our position."

I didn't know it then, but twenty-five months later, when the tribunal delivered a ninety-one-page analysing every aspect of this case—from contract interpretation to witness credibility to whether time was fundamental—these words would be nowhere in it.

Not mentioned. Not explained. Not reconciled with the tribunal's claim that they'd carefully considered our defence before reaching their decision.

As if they'd never been said.

* * * *

And then came Mr Doe.

John Doe was the Company's key witness on operations. He'd been involved in the actual conduct of the covert military activities. His testimony was critical to their case.

And his "two new paragraphs" turned out to be much more than that.

Under examination by the Company's counsel, Doe spent approximately twenty-five pages of transcript attacking Jack Wayne. Wayne had been the chief executive officer of the subcontractor the

Company had hired to conduct the operations. We had submitted numerous documents written by Wayne—emails, memos, letters—that described the Company's failures to deliver equipment, their disorganisation, and their inability to perform.

Those documents were devastating to the Company's case. They were contemporaneous, detailed, and written by someone within the Company's operations. They showed that the equipment hadn't been delivered, that the Company had failed to perform, and that the Company's failures had compromised the operation.

So, Doe's strategy—the purpose of those "two new paragraphs"—was to destroy Wayne's credibility.

He claimed Wayne had misappropriated funds. He claimed Wayne had written those documents in bad faith, trying to take over the contract for himself. He claimed Wayne was motivated not by truth but by greed and ambition.

It was a comprehensive character assassination. And it was completely new—nothing like this had been in the original witness statement we'd received weeks earlier.

The presiding arbitrator interrupted at one point. "You don't have this in your statement. You don't have it in your statement on oath. You've said quite a few things against Wayne. For the first time, you are now making these allegations which you have not made in your statement on oath?"

For a moment, I thought the presiding arbitrator might actually stop this. Might enforce the rules about witness statements and proper disclosure.

But then the Company's counsel responded, and the presiding arbitrator let it continue.

Twenty-five pages of testimony attacking a man who wasn't present, who hadn't been called as a witness, who had no opportunity to defend himself. All based on allegations that had been introduced at the hearing without advance notice.

I didn't object to Doe's line of testimony—I didn't construct our defence around Wayne's crucial documents, even though they detailed the Company's failures to deliver equipment, its disorganisation, and its inability to perform the contract as constituted. I allowed the Company's counsel to go on a wild-goose chase, far from the defence I had constructed.

I cross-examined Doe as best I could. But without notice, without time to prepare, without the ability to call Wayne as a rebuttal witness, I was fighting with one hand tied behind my back.

And that, I believed, was the strategic purpose. The Company waited until the hearing to introduce this attack on Wayne, knowing we wouldn't have time to respond effectively.

* * * *

After the first day of testimony, my team and I returned to the hotel.

"They ambushed us," one of my lawyers said. "Twenty-five pages attacking Wayne, none of it disclosed in advance. How are we supposed to respond to that?"

"We respond afterwards," I said. "The tribunal reserved our right. We'll try to find and submit a rebuttal statement from Wayne. We'll call witnesses who can attest to his character. We'll request that Doe be recalled for cross-examination on this new material."

"Will the tribunal allow it?"

I thought about that. The tribunal had shown a pattern of accommodating the Company while denying our procedural requests. But they'd made a commitment at the hearing. They'd said we could respond. They'd said the hearing could continue for that purpose.

"They'll have to," I said. "Because if they don't, it will be such an obvious denial of fair hearing that any they issue will be vulnerable to challenge."

But even as I said it, I wondered. This tribunal had already made so many decisions that departed from the rules and standard practice. Would one more really matter to them?

* * * *

The Company finished its case on August 3. We had the weekend to prepare before our defence began on August 8.

During those days off, I focused my team on two things: preparing our witnesses for testimony and developing our strategy to rebut Doe's allegations.

But I also spent time alone, thinking about the eureka argument still held in reserve. The staged contract theory that explained why the Company's claims were baseless, regardless of any testimony given at this hearing.

The Company had presented their case. They'd claimed they'd performed. They'd claimed they were owed three billion dollars. They'd attacked our evidence and our witnesses.

But they hadn't addressed—they couldn't address—the fundamental flaw in their case because they didn't yet know we'd identified it.

The contract was staged. It had been terminated before the later stages could be performed. They were claiming payment for work never done.

And I would explain all of that in the post-hearing brief after this hearing was over. After they'd committed to their positions. After it was too late for them to adjust.

* * * *

August 8 arrived—time for our defence.

We called three witnesses over two days. Colonel Fade testified first, via ZOOM—he was unable to travel to Abuja. He described the operations, the equipment that had been promised, paid for and never delivered, the Company's failures and the execution of the settlement agreement.

The presiding arbitrator's questions during Fade's testimony were sceptical, probing, and challenging. Not the supportive, clarifying questions he'd asked the Company's witnesses, but constructive cross-examination—noticeably different in tone from the questions he'd asked the Company's witnesses.

Colonel Ashley testified in person on August 8 and 9. His testimony was critical—he'd been directly involved in the operations, had witnessed the Company's failures, and had seen the settlement negotiations.

Ashley first testified to what had actually been delivered versus what had been paid for. He'd calculated the differential—compared contract obligations to documentary evidence of delivery. His numbers showed Nigeria had overpaid.

The Company's counsel attacked his calculations. Suggested he was inflating Nigeria's payment, minimising the Company's deliveries.

The presiding arbitrator took notes but said nothing.

Twenty-five months later, the Award would confirm Ashley's calculations almost exactly. The tribunal would find Nigeria had overpaid by US$2,865,769.37—nearly three million dollars more than the first milestone payment required.

Ashley had been right. The documentary evidence had been clear. Nigeria had paid more than the contract demanded and received less than the contract promised.

But at the hearing, none of that seemed to matter. The tribunal had "formed their impression." They'd made up their minds.

Or so I thought. So it seemed from the presiding arbitrator's comments.

* * * *

During Colonel Ashley's testimony, we delved into what I believed was one of our strongest defences: the settlement agreement itself.

The Company's entire case rested on the claim that they'd been coerced into signing the End of Contract and Closure Agreement in April 2015, that the government had forced them to accept US$8.8 million and walk away from a contract they claimed they were owed three billion dollars and that Mr George Sweeny had signed under duress, with no choice, facing professional and financial ruin.

It was a compelling narrative. A small contractor bullied by a powerful government. David versus Goliath. The kind of story that arbitrators might find sympathetic.

Except it wasn't true.

Except that the documentary evidence told a different story.

And I could prove it with their own documents.

* * * *

When Colonel Ashley took the stand on August 8, I walked him through the actual sequence of events leading to the settlement. Not the dramatic story the Company had told, but what had really happened, documented in emails and payment records.

"Colonel," I said, "when did the contract operation actually end?"

"The subcontractor—ATTEP—terminated their agreement with the Company on March 18, 2015," Ashley said. "They withdrew their forces on March 30. At that point, the operation was over. The Company had no capacity to continue."

"And after that, who initiated contact about ending the contract?"

"Mr Sweeny did. He approached us with a proposal."

I pulled up Exhibit R-19 on the screen—an email from Sweeny to Ashley dated early April 2015.

"What was in this proposal?"

"He wanted to modify the contract. Offer just airwing operations instead of the full package. And he offered to sell us the REVA vehicles—the armoured trucks—for US$3.4 million."

"Did the government accept this proposal?"

"No. But we made a counteroffer."

I displayed Exhibit R-20— Ashley's response email, dated a few days later.

"What was your counteroffer?"

"We offered US$5.8 million total. That included purchasing the REVA vehicles he'd offered to sell, paying for outstanding arms shipments from China and Bulgaria, and covering the freight costs for delivery."

"And how did Mr Sweeny respond to this counteroffer?"

Ashley smiled slightly. "He was satisfied with it."

I pulled up Exhibit R-21— Sweeny's email response, dated April 4, 2015. I read it aloud to the tribunal:

"'The proposal is indeed a clean break; I assume then our air wing will not be required to return? It's all fair, and this will cover all remaining expenses, which was my biggest worry.'"

I let that sit for a moment. "He said it was 'all fair'?"

"Yes."

"And that it would 'cover all remaining expenses'—his 'biggest worry'?"

"That's what he wrote."

"Did he express any concern about being pressured or coerced?"

"No. He was satisfied. In fact, two days later, he sent a letter of appreciation to the National Security Adviser."

I displayed Exhibit R-22—the letter dated April 6, 2015. Sweeny thanked the NSA for the opportunity to serve, for the settlement arrangement, expressing gratitude.

"A letter of appreciation," I repeated. "Thanking the government for the settlement, he now claims he was forced to accept under duress."

The presiding arbitrator was taking notes, but his expression gave nothing away.

"When was the settlement agreement actually signed?" I asked.

"April 29, 2015."

"And when was the money paid?"

"Most of it was paid before the signing. US$3.4 million on April 10 for the vehicles. US$2.15 million on April 15 for the arms shipments. That's US$5.55 million paid before Mr Sweeny ever signed the agreement."

I paused to let the tribunal absorb that. The Company claimed they'd been handed cash and an agreement and forced to sign on the spot. But the evidence showed they'd received most of the money weeks earlier.

"What happened after those payments?" I asked.

"Mr Sweeny came back and complained. Said he wasn't making any profit on the deal. Even though we weren't legally obligated to pay him anything more, the NSA authorised an additional US$3 million as a final settlement."

"So, the government increased the settlement amount after Mr Sweeny complained?"

"Yes. To US$8.8 million total."

"And then the agreement was signed?"

"Yes, on April 29."

"Who was present at that signing?"

"Col. Fade coordinated it. Mr Sweeny and Mr James Black were there on behalf of the Company. Our Director of Finance witnessed."

"Were you present?"

"No. I was in my office. They signed it and brought it to me afterwards."

This was critical. The Company had claimed at this hearing that you had threatened Sweeny, told him to, "sign or get nothing." But Ashley hadn't even been in the room.

* * * *

During cross-examination, the Company's counsel tried to suggest that the negotiations had been one-sided.

"But you were representing the government," counsel said. "A powerful entity. And Mr Sweeny was just one man with a small company."

"We negotiated in good faith," Ashley said. "Mr Sweeny proposed. We made a counteroffer. He accepted. Then he asked for more money, and we gave it to him. That's not coercion—that's negotiation."

"But he had no choice—"

"He had a choice. He could have rejected our offer. He could have walked away. Instead, he said it was 'all fair' and sent us a thank-you letter."

The Company's counsel moved on quickly.

But then the presiding arbitrator interjected with something that echoed what he'd said during the Company's case: "Many of what you are trying to establish now we have formed our impression about it."

Formed our impression before hearing our case, our defence in full.

I looked at my team. The pattern was unmistakable. During the Company's case, when we were cross-examining Sweeny, the tribunal already had "a position." Now, during our defence, during Ashley's cross-examination, they had "formed our impression."

The transcript would capture this too. Two announcements of pre-judgment, made in open proceedings, recorded word-for-word.

"We have our position." "We've formed our impression."

The tribunal was telling us—telling the record—that our defence wouldn't change anything. That they'd already decided.

But they'd still take twenty-five months to write the Award. Twenty-five months after announcing they'd already formed their views. And in those ninety-one pages, they'd never explain what they'd meant. Never address the contradiction between prejudging and deliberating. Never mention these statements at all.

The pattern wasn't just in the decisions. It was in what they were willing to say out loud.

Even the Lord Almighty gave Adam a hearing before judgment. But this tribunal had apparently formed views before hearing our full case.

* * * *

When we recalled Colonel Fade via ZOOM the next day, I asked him about the actual signing.

"Colonel, please describe what happened on April 29 when the settlement agreement was signed."

"I gave them three copies of the agreement," Fade said. "I told them to review everything carefully. I left the room to give them privacy. When I came back, they'd reviewed it and were ready to sign."

"Did you pressure them in any way?"

"Of course not. They came requesting this settlement. We wanted to accommodate them."

"Did anyone threaten Mr Sweeny?"

"No."

"Did Colonel Ashley threaten him?"

"Col. Ashley wasn't even there. He was in his office."

"Did Mr Sweeny express any objection to the terms?"

"None. He signed willingly."

The Company's counsel cross-examined aggressively, but Fade was unshakeable. No threats. No coercion. Just a negotiated settlement initiated and accepted by the Company.

* * * *

But the most damaging evidence wasn't the negotiations or the signing—it was what happened afterwards.

I walked Ashley through the delivery records. After signing the settlement and receiving all US$8.8 million, the Company continued to fulfil its terms for 10 months.

"What did the settlement agreement require the Company to do?" I asked.

"Complete the shipment of outstanding arms and ammunition from Bulgaria and China. Deliver the equipment they'd been paid to deliver."

"And did they do that?"

"Yes. For almost a year afterwards."

I displayed the documents one by one:

- May 8, 2015: Delivery receipt for pistols to Nigerian Armed Forces. Two weeks after signing.
- June 26, 2015: Delivery certificate for ammunition. Two months after signing.
- August 11, 2015: Air waybill for cartridges. Four months after signing.
- October 21, 2015: Air waybill for machine gun barrels. Six months after signing.
- February 9, 2016: Confirmation of delivery for ammunition. Ten months after signing.

* * * *

"They were still delivering equipment ten months later?" I asked.

"Yes."

"If Mr Sweeny had been coerced into signing this agreement, if he'd signed under duress as he claims now, would you expect him to comply with its terms for ten months afterwards voluntarily?"

"No. If someone forces you to sign something against your will, you don't voluntarily perform it for a year."

The presiding arbitrator interrupted. "These deliveries—were they made in Nigeria?"

"Yes, sir. Mr Sweeny arranged the shipments, coordinated with our forces, and ensured delivery. He voluntarily fulfilled the settlement terms long after any alleged pressure had ended."

During Ashley's cross-examination, something remarkable happened. The presiding arbitrator suggested—not asked, but suggested—that the contract had been a lease agreement.

"The equipment was leased, wasn't it?" the presiding arbitrator said. Not to clarify, but as if stating a fact.

"No, sir," Ashley responded. "The contract was for procurement. Some equipment was to be purchased, some leased from third parties, but it wasn't a lease contract with the Company."

The presiding arbitrator pressed. "But there were lease arrangements?"

"For some equipment, yes, but—"

"So, it was a lease."

I could see what was happening. The presiding arbitrator was trying to establish that the contract was primarily a lease agreement. Because if it were a lease, then the Company's claim for lease rental fees might seem more plausible.

But it wasn't a lease. It was a staged procurement and performance contract. And the presiding arbitrator's characterisation was concerning. If the contract were characterised as a lease, the Company would become the owner of the equipment and be entitled to lease rentals, the return of the remaining equipment, or their monetary equivalent—the very relief the Company was seeking.

What happened at that moment appeared to go beyond clarification to substantive suggestions about the case.

We continued presenting our case because we had no choice. At that moment, I had serious concerns that the tribunal had pre-judged the outcome. The statement suggested they had formed conclusions before hearing all the evidence.

The only question now was whether the post-hearing brief—with arguments they hadn't anticipated, with logic they couldn't escape—could give them reason to reconsider preliminary views they appeared to have formed.

* * * *

I made a note in my pad: *Presiding arbitrator characterising the contract as a lease. Attempting to establish a legal theory favourable to the Company.*

The presiding arbitrator was characterising the contract. Not asking about it. Characterising it.

A procurement contract—under which Nigeria paid for equipment and services—was being recharacterized as a lease. As if Nigeria had borrowed equipment, it should return. As if the Company's failure to deliver on time didn't matter because Nigeria was merely leasing, not purchasing.

This wasn't a question seeking clarification. This was a legal theory. One that would excuse the Company's timeline failures and create an ongoing obligation for Nigeria to pay—or return equipment that had never arrived on schedule.

I made a note. Added it to the pattern.

The tribunal had its "position" on the facts. They'd "formed their impression" on the evidence. And now they were suggesting a legal characterisation that would support the Company's claim.

The transcript would capture this too. Every word. Every suggestion. Every statement that revealed how they were approaching the case.

Twenty-five months later, the tribunal would adopt a completely different characterisation. The tribunal would call the contract "STAGED"—multiple phases contingent on delivery and performance. They'd agree that payment for each stage depended on completion of the prior stage. They'd find that time was fundamental.

They'd reject the lease theory entirely. Accept our staged contract analysis. Adopt the framework from our post-hearing brief word-for-word.

But they'd never explain what the presiding arbitrator had meant when he suggested, during the hearing, that it was a lease. Never reconcile that suggestion with their ultimate finding. Never acknowledge the inconsistency.

The record would show one thing. The Award would say another. And the gap between them would simply... disappear.

* * * *

After Ashley finished, we called the Special Assistant who'd been supporting us throughout the case. He testified about the government's position, about the settlement negotiations, and about the Company's conduct.

By the end of August 9, we'd presented our defence. Our witnesses had testified. Our documents had been introduced. Our case had been made.

But I hadn't deployed the eureka argument. I'd presented strong evidence—the settlement agreement, the payment records, the Company's failures. But I'd saved the key legal theory for later. It was the winning argument.

It was a calculated decision: deploy the winning argument when it was too late to counter.

* * * *

During our closing arguments on the final day, I addressed the duress claim directly.

"The Company wants this tribunal to believe that Mr Sweeny was coerced into signing the settlement agreement," I said. "That he had no choice. That he signed under duress, facing threats and intimidation.

"But the evidence tells a different story.

"Mr Sweeny initiated the settlement negotiations. He proposed terms. The government made a counteroffer. He responded in writing that it was 'all fair' and would cover his expenses. He sent a thank-you letter to the National Security Adviser expressing gratitude.

"The government paid him US$5.55 million before he ever signed the agreement. Then, after he complained, they paid him an additional US$3.25 million—money they had no legal obligation to pay.

"He signed the agreement after reviewing it privately, with no one pressuring him, with Colonel Ashley not even present in the room.

"And then, for ten months afterwards, he voluntarily complied with its terms. Continued to deliver equipment and continued to fulfil his obligations under an agreement he now claims was forced upon him.

"That is not duress. That is not coercion. That is a freely negotiated settlement that the Company accepted, benefited from, and performed under—until they decided, years later, that they wanted three billion dollars instead.

"The settlement agreement is valid and binding. It represents the parties' mutual agreement to end the contract amicably. And it should be upheld."

The presiding arbitrator made notes but said nothing.

* * * *

After presenting our substantive arguments on the merits, there remained one procedural matter to address.

I stood to address the tribunal.

"Sir, with respect to the new allegations introduced by Mr Doe at this hearing, allegations that were not disclosed in advance, I would like to reserve the right to submit a rebuttal. The Company introduced twenty-five pages of new testimony attacking Mr Wayne, who is not a party to these proceedings and had no opportunity to respond. I request the opportunity to submit Mr Wayne's sworn statement in response, and to recall Mr Doe for cross-examination on this new material."

The presiding arbitrator nodded. "That right is reserved. You may submit your application for continuation of the hearing after you've had time to prepare your rebuttal materials."

"Thank you, sir."

The hearing was adjourned. Not closed—adjourned. We would submit post-hearing briefs. There might be further proceedings for my rebuttal to Doe. But the evidentiary hearing itself—the testimony, the cross-examinations—was complete.

* * * *

That evening, back at the hotel, my team and I debriefed.

"How do you think it went?" one of them asked.

"We presented our case well," I said. "Our witnesses were credible. Our evidence was strong. The settlement agreement is unassailable."

"But the tribunal..."

"The tribunal's conduct was consistent with the pattern we'd been documenting. Differential treatment favouring the Company. Sceptical treatment of our case. The presiding arbitrator characterised the contract as a lease. He interrupted our witnesses. He helped their witnesses. None of that is surprising."

"So, what happens now?"

"Now we go back to Lagos. We begin to craft our post-hearing brief. We find and convince Wayne to participate and defend his integrity, and if he agrees, we submit his statement and request to recall Doe. And we wait to see if the tribunal grants that request."

"And if they don't?"

"Then we document that too. Another procedural decision to document. Another concern about fair process. Another data point in the pattern we'd been recording."

One of my lawyers said, "The settlement evidence was strong. Really strong. Sweeny's own emails, the thank-you letter, the continued performance—it all contradicts their duress claim."

"It does," I agreed.

"Do you think the tribunal will accept it?"

I thought about the past three years. The pattern of decisions. The procedural irregularities. The presiding arbitrator's attempt to characterise the contract as a lease.

"In a typical tribunal or with different arbitrators, this evidence would be dispositive," I said. "No reasonable arbitrator could look at those emails—'it's all fair,' the thank-you letter, ten months of voluntary performance—and conclude there was duress."

"But we're concerned about the pattern we've observed."

"Yes," I said. "We are."

"So, what do we do?"

"We do what we've always done. We build the record. We present the evidence. We make the arguments. And we document every irregularity, every prejudice, every deviation from proper procedure. Because if this tribunal rules against us despite this evidence, that ruling won't survive scrutiny."

But privately, I was thinking about the post-hearing brief and about the staged contract argument, still waiting to be deployed. About how all of this—the settlement evidence, the delivery records, the Company's own admissions—would fit together in that final, devastating analysis.

The settlement agreement was strong evidence. But it wasn't the eureka argument.

That was still coming.

And when it did, the tribunal would have to confront the mathematical impossibility of the Company's three-billion-dollar claim.

The hearing was over. But the real fight was just beginning.

And I was ready.

One of the senior lawyers—the one who'd become closest to me over three years—shared information he gathered during the hearing that explained certain difficulties we'd encountered throughout the case.

"I've learned something that clarifies why we've had such limited institutional support," he said carefully.

He referred to institutional coordination challenges and professional relationships that, in his view, may have contributed to those difficulties. He did not allege misconduct or impropriety, and I do not make any such allegation here. I have chosen not to detail these matters further because they were not determinative of the merits, but they explain a great deal.

I understood immediately what he was suggesting. The lack of documentation. The unavailable witnesses. The minimal coordination from certain government offices despite the magnitude of the claim.

"Does this change anything?" another team member asked.

"No," I said. "We're still going to prevail. We're still going to write the brief that presents evidence the tribunal cannot reasonably disregard. But it explains why this case has felt like fighting alone."

I immediately informed the Special Assistant about these concerns. He later confirmed that they had indeed verified institutional complications affecting the government's coordination in the case.

* * * *

The hearing ended on August 9, 2022. Nine days of testimony. Hundreds of exhibits. A complete record of everything that had been said—including what the tribunal had revealed about their pre-judgment.

"We have our position."
"We've formed our impression."
"The equipment was leased, wasn't it?"

All of it captured by the court reporter. All of it preserved in the transcript. All of it part of the official record of the proceedings.

I'd challenged the arbitrators under Article 13 of the UNCITRAL Rules. That challenge was in the record. I'd documented every differential ruling, every decision that favoured the Company, every statement that revealed pre-judgment. That documentation was in the record.

The tribunal had rejected my challenge. They'd ruled they could continue serving. That ruling was in the record too.

Now we'd write our post-hearing brief. We'd make our case so compelling that the tribunal would have to rule in our favour—even if they'd already decided against us.

The brief would go into the record. The Company's inability to respond would go into the record. And eventually, the Award would go into the record.

But I was beginning to understand something about records in arbitration.

A record is only as complete as those with power want it to be.

The transcript might capture pre-judgment statements. The Award might omit it.

The proceedings might show preferential treatment. The official account might erase it.

You can document everything. Preserve everything. Build a perfect record of every impropriety.

And in the end, when the tribunal writes becomes the authoritative account of what happened—when they're reviewing their own conduct, writing their own history—the record becomes whatever they say it is.

That's not a flaw in the system.

That's the system working exactly as designed.

Chapter 9

The Rebuttal

The flight back to Lagos on August 10 should have felt like relief. Nine days of testimony, cross-examination, and challenging tribunal interactions were behind us. We'd presented our case. The settlement agreement evidence was strong. And we had the eureka argument waiting in reserve for the post-hearing brief.

But I couldn't stop thinking about John Doe’s twenty-five-page testimony.

What follows describes my contemporaneous understanding of the tribunal’s procedural decisions, assessed cumulatively from the standpoint of a party participant based on the record as it appeared to me at the time.

Twenty-five pages attacking Jack Wayne. Twenty-five pages of character assassination introduced at the hearing without notice. Twenty-five pages claiming Wayne had written his devastating emails and memos—the documents proving the Company's failures—not to tell the truth, but to steal the contract for himself.

If the tribunal believed Doe, they could dismiss Wayne’s documents as self-serving lies. And those documents were crucial to our case. They were contemporaneous, detailed, and written by someone inside the

Company's operations. They showed the equipment hadn't been delivered, that timelines had been missed, and that the Company had failed to perform.

Wayne's documents weren't just helpful evidence—they were contemporaneous internal communications written by the CEO of ATTEP during the operation itself. Emails to his own team. Memos to his directors. Reports written in real time as events unfolded, when memories were fresh, and there was no litigation to shade the truth.

In litigation or arbitration, contemporaneous documents carry special weight. They're written before anyone knows there will be a dispute, before anyone has reason to shade the facts. As one English judge put it, they're "the documents where a witness's guard is down, and their true thoughts are plain to see."

Wayne had written these documents to his own people—internal communications describing the Company's failures to deliver equipment, the delays, the disorganisation. If what he'd written wasn't true, his own team would have challenged him at the time. But they hadn't. The documents stood unchallenged, contemporaneous proof of what had actually happened.

That's what made Doe's attack so dangerous. If the tribunal believed Wayne had written those documents in bad faith—motivated by greed rather than truth—they could dismiss the most powerful evidence in our case.

Even though our defence wasn't constructed on Wayne's documents, we couldn't let Doe's allegations stand unchallenged.

The tribunal had reserved our right to respond. They'd said we could submit rebuttal evidence. They'd even suggested we could recall Doe for further cross-examination. And at the cost of the Company that introduced the evidence at the hearing.

* * * *

But to do that effectively, I needed Jack Wayne himself.

Finding Wayne wasn't going to be easy.

He was the former CEO of ATTEP—Advanced Tasks, Training, Equipment and Protection—the South African firm the Company had subcontracted to conduct the actual military operations. ATTEP had provided the foreign soldiers, the operational expertise, and the combat leadership. They'd been on the ground in Nigeria from December 2014 through March 2015, when they'd terminated their contract with the Company and withdrawn.

Wayne had written extensive documentation during that period. Emails to his team. Memos to the Company. Letters explaining delays, equipment failures, and coordination problems. We'd got access to these documents and had submitted them as exhibits in our defence. They were strong evidence of the Company's incompetence and failures to perform.

* * * *

But Wayne wasn't our witness. He'd worked for the Company, not the government. The Company had paid his firm. He'd defended the Company in public and had been critical of the government. As far as any normal analysis would suggest, he should be hostile to us.

And yet, his documents told our story better than our own witnesses could.

The Special Assistant didn't want me to contact him. But I needed to correct the impression the damaging character testimony had left on the arbitrators.

I'd never met Wayne and never spoken to him. He'd operated in a covert world where government lawyers didn't intrude. By the time I'd taken this case in 2019, he'd been out of Nigeria for 4 years.

But I needed him now.

Government representatives advised against contacting him—they said he is an adversary and will be hostile to our interests.

But I thought otherwise—Wayne would like to clear his name with the level of accusations against him by John Doe.

* * * *

On Monday, August 15, back in my Lagos office, I began the search.

ATTEP was still operational—I found their website easily enough. But getting Wayne's contact information specifically proved difficult. The firm's public presence was minimal, by design. Private military contractors don't advertise.

I reached out through professional networks. Colleagues who'd worked in security consulting. Lawyers who'd handled military contracts. Anyone who might have a connection to South African private military circles.

Three days later, I had an email address. Not Wayne's directly, but someone at ATTEP who could pass along a message.

I drafted the email carefully:

Mr. Wayne,

My name is Andy Oji. I represent the Federal Government of Nigeria in an arbitration brought by [the Company]. You don't know me, but your name came up extensively at the recent hearing.

Mr John Doe, testifying for the Company, spent approximately twenty-five pages of transcript attacking your character and credibility. He alleged that the emails and memos you wrote during your time in Nigeria—documents that describe the Company's failures—were written not to report the truth, but because you wanted to take over the contract for yourself.

I'm writing to ask whether you'd be willing to provide a sworn statement addressing these allegations. The tribunal has reserved our right to submit rebuttal evidence. Your statement could be crucial to the case.

I've attached the relevant portions of Doe's testimony for your review.

I hesitated before hitting send. This was asking a lot. Wayne had no obligation to help us. He'd moved on with his life. Getting involved in an arbitration years after the fact, defending himself against allegations he'd probably never heard—why would he agree?

But I sent it anyway.

Two days passed with no response.

Then, on August 20, my phone rang. A South African number.

"Mr Oji, this is Jack Wayne."

His voice was measured, controlled—a military bearing even over the phone. But I could hear something else underneath. Anger. Jack Wayne was a retired General.

"I read what Doe said about me."

"I'm sorry you had to see that," I said. "It was sprung on us at the hearing. We had no advance notice that he was going to make those allegations."

"Financial misappropriation. Taking over the contract. Writing reports in bad faith." His voice was tight. "Twenty-five pages of lies, and I wasn't even there to defend myself."

"That's why I'm reaching out. The tribunal gave us the right to respond. If you're willing to provide a statement—"

"I'll do it," he said immediately. "What do you need?"

We spent the next hour on the phone. I walked him through what had happened at the hearing, the procedural posture, and what a witness statement should include. He listened, asked sharp questions, and understood immediately what was at stake.

"Everything I wrote was true," he said. "Every email, every memo. I documented the Company's failures because that's what happened. They didn't deliver the equipment. They didn't follow the timelines. They were disorganised and incompetent. And when I reported these problems, Sweeny didn't want to hear it."

"Can you prove that in a statement?"

"I can prove all of it. I have records. Communications. Documentation from the time. Doe says I wanted to take over the contract? I terminated our contract and walked away. If I'd wanted to take over, I would have stayed."

"How quickly can you prepare a statement?"

"Give me a week. I'll have something for you by next Friday."

After we hung up, I sat in my office feeling something I hadn't felt in weeks. Hope.

Wayne wasn't just willing to help. He was motivated. Angry at being falsely accused. Determined to set the record straight.

And he had documentation to back up everything he'd say.

* * * *

While waiting for Wayne's statement, I focused on the other element of our rebuttal: finding additional witnesses who could vouch for his character.

Doe had attacked Wayne personally. Called his integrity into question. Suggested he was motivated by greed rather than truth. We needed people who'd worked with Wayne, who could testify to his professionalism and honesty.

I reached out to Wayne again. "Who else from ATTEP was in Nigeria during the operation? People who witnessed what happened. People who can confirm your version of events."

He gave me four names:

Frank Smith John. Operations officer. On the ground in Maiduguri during the combat phase.

Paul Tommy Mbugua. Logistics coordinator. Witnessed the equipment delivery failures.

Anthony Johnson Simiyu. Training officer. Based at the Jaji training facility.

Jadon Joshua Kanani. Administrative support. Handled communications between ATTEP and the Company.

All four had worked directly with Wayne. All four had seen the Company's failures firsthand. And all four, Wayne assured me, would be willing to provide statements.

"They're good men," he said. "Professionals. They saw what I saw. They know what I wrote was true."

Over the next week, I interviewed and coordinated with each of them. Explained the situation. Sent them drafts of witness statements to review and modify. Worked with them to ensure their testimony was precise, factual, and compelling.

By September 8, I had completed all four statements. Each one corroborated Wayne's account. Each one described the Company's failures. Each one vouched for Wayne's integrity and professionalism.

In addition to Wayne's own statement, we had four witnesses ready to demolish Doe's allegations.

* * * *

Wayne’s statement arrived on August 26—twenty-five pages, matching Doe's testimony page for page.

I read it immediately, and as I turned each page, my confidence grew.

It was devastating.

Wayne walked through his entire involvement with the project—the initial contract with the Company. The promises made about equipment and support. The reality of what actually arrived—late, incomplete, inadequate.

He addressed Doe's allegations directly. Financial misappropriation? Here were the accounting records showing every dollar properly spent and documented. Trying to take over the contract? Here was ATTEP's termination letter, withdrawing from the project due to the Company's failure to provide necessary support.

But more importantly, he explained why he'd written those critical emails and memos during the operation. Not to undermine the Company, but to document problems that were putting lives at risk. Equipment that hadn't arrived. Ammunition that was delayed. Vehicles that broke down because spare parts weren't available.

"I had soldiers in the field," Wayne wrote. "My responsibility was to their safety and mission success. When the Company failed to provide what they'd promised, I documented it. Not to take over the contract, but to protect my people and ensure the operation could continue."

The statement included dozens of supporting exhibits. Emails. Invoices. Delivery records. Communication logs. Everything timestamped, contemporary, verifiable.

It was exactly what we needed.

Wayne's statement did something else crucial: it established that his original documents were exactly what they appeared to be—honest, contemporaneous reporting.

He walked through when each document was written, who received it, and why. The emails to his team describing equipment delays? Written immediately after those delays occurred, copied to multiple ATTEP personnel who were witnessing the same problems. The memos about the Company's failures? Internal communications to his own directors, not documents prepared for outside consumption.

And here was the key point: when Wayne had written those critical assessments in early 2015, none of his ATTEP colleagues had contradicted him. Not Doe. Not anyone. They'd received his emails, read his memos, and said nothing—because what he'd written was true, and they all knew it.

Under the law, silence in response to business correspondence is acceptance. When Doe received Wayne's emails describing the Company's failures and didn't respond, didn't object, didn't correct—he accepted their truth. That acceptance was in the record, preserved in the metadata of unreplied emails.

Now, seven years later, Doe wanted to claim those same documents were lies. But he'd had his chance to challenge them in 2015, when they were written, when the facts were fresh. He hadn't. That silence was damning.

* * * *

On August 27, I submitted our application to the tribunal.

The letter was direct: We were requesting continuation of the hearing. We'd submit Wayne’s statement immediately, with additional witness statements to follow. We were requesting that the tribunal recall John Doe for cross-examination on his new allegations.

I cited the UNCITRAL Rules. Article 17(3): parties have the right to present evidence through witnesses. Article 31(1): The hearing isn't closed until the tribunal declares it closed.

The tribunal had ended the hearing on August 9. They hadn't declared it closed. They'd explicitly reserved our right to respond. This wasn't reopening anything—this was a continuation of a hearing that remained in progress.

I sent the letter by email and courier to all three arbitrators and the Company's counsel.

Then I waited.

* * * *

The Company's response arrived on August 30.

Counsel for the Company objected to our application. The hearing was complete, they argued. Both parties had presented their cases. The Respondent had closed its case on August 9. There was no basis to bring additional witnesses at this time.

As for Doe's testimony, they claimed it wasn't really "new." The allegations had been known since 2021, they said. The fact that Doe had expanded on them at the hearing didn't change anything.

It was exactly the kind of bad-faith argument I'd come to expect from the Company's counsel. They'd ambushed us with new allegations at the hearing, and now they were claiming we'd had plenty of time to respond.

I drafted our reply on September 5.

The tone was measured but firm. This wasn't an application to reopen the hearing—the hearing had never been closed. The tribunal had specifically told us we could respond. The Company's counsel had even acknowledged at the hearing that we might need "a right to reply."

I included a transcript excerpt from August 1, showing the presiding arbitrator's exact words: "If you have any serious objection... we will have the opportunity of getting him back on a remote hearing if you feel that you need to cross-examine him."

The tribunal had promised us this opportunity. We were simply taking them up on it.

* * * *

On September 8, I submitted the four additional witness statements—John, Mbugua, Simiyu and Kanani.

Five witnesses in total. Twenty-five pages from Wayne, plus supporting statements from four men who'd worked alongside him. All of them corroborated the same story: the Company had failed to perform, Wayne had documented that failure truthfully, and Doe's allegations were false.

It was a comprehensive rebuttal. The strongest response we could possibly provide.

My team and I discussed it in our daily meeting that afternoon.

"This should be overwhelming," one of them said. "Five witnesses against Doe's unsupported allegations. Contemporary documents. Verifiable facts."

"In a fair, independent and impartial tribunal, it would be," I agreed.

"You think they'll reject it?"

I thought about the pattern we'd documented over three years. The systematic indulgence. The favouritism toward the Company. The procedural irregularities. The pattern of procedural decisions. The differential treatment towards the Company.

"I think they'll find a reason," I said. Based on the pattern of prior procedural rulings, I was concerned they would find a technical basis to accept Doe's late testimony while rejecting a structured rebuttal.

"Then why are we doing this?"

"Because we have to try. Because it's the right response. We've got to do what we've got to do—at least for the record. And because when they reject it, we'll have another piece of evidence documenting their impartiality."

The lawyer closest to me said quietly, "You're building a record for after the Award. For challenging it if they rule against us."

"Yes," I admitted. "That's exactly what I'm doing."

* * * *

The tribunal's ruling arrived on September 23, two weeks after I'd submitted the final witness statements.

I opened it with a sense of foreboding that proved entirely justified.

The tribunal rejected the four additional witnesses outright. John, Mbugua, Simiyu and Kanani—all of them excluded. Their witness statements would not be accepted. Their testimony would not be heard.

As for Wayne, the tribunal would accept his statement, but with severe limitations. He could only address the specific two paragraphs that Doe had added to his written statement. He could not respond to the twenty-five pages of testimony Doe had given at the hearing.

The reasoning was technical and procedural, and, in my view, completely wrong.

The tribunal claimed we were trying to "reopen" the hearing, which required showing "exceptional circumstances." They cited a Nigerian court case about recalling witnesses—a case about civil procedure in Nigerian courts, not international arbitration under UNCITRAL Rules.

But we hadn't asked to reopen anything. The hearing had never been closed. The tribunal had adjourned it. They'd reserved our right to respond. We were simply continuing a hearing that remained in progress.

I read through the ruling twice, making notes.

The tribunal claimed both parties had "closed their cases" on August 9. But I hadn't closed our case—I'd specifically told them I intended to respond to Doe's new allegations.

They claimed we should have submitted our rebuttal during the hearing. But Wayne wasn't at our "beck and call." I needed time to contact him, explain the situation, and prepare a proper response.

They claimed the issue was merely two paragraphs in Doe's statement. But those two paragraphs had been the gateway to twenty-five pages of testimony—testimony the presiding arbitrator himself had questioned during the hearing.

The ruling was dated September 23. In my view, it was wrong on the facts, wrong on the procedure, wrong in common sense and wrong on the law.

But it was also final.

The ruling was particularly troubling given the nature of Wayne's evidence. These weren't just ordinary witness statements—they were supported by contemporaneous internal documents written during the operation itself. Documents that courts and tribunals typically regard as far more reliable than testimony given years later, after disputes have hardened and memories have faded.

Courts and tribunal around the world have repeatedly emphasised this principle: contemporaneous documents are "of the utmost importance" precisely because they're created before anyone knows litigation will follow, before anyone has a motive to shade the truth.

Wayne's documents had that quality. Internal ATTEP communications. Real-time reports. Emails to his own team describing what was happening on the ground. If those documents had been inaccurate, his colleagues would have challenged them immediately. But Doe—who'd received many of those emails—had never responded, never objected, never corrected.

Under legal principles recognised across common law jurisdictions, the failure to respond to business correspondence constituted acceptance of their contents. Doe had, in effect, acknowledged the truth of Wayne's reports by his silence in 2015.

Now the tribunal was preventing Wayne from explaining that silence. Preventing him from walking through the contemporaneous record. Limiting his testimony to two paragraphs while allowing Doe's twenty-five pages of belated attack to stand unchallenged.

* * * *

I called an emergency meeting with my team that afternoon.

"They rejected four of our five witnesses," I told them. "And they've limited Wayne to responding only to two paragraphs, not the twenty-five pages of testimony."

The exhaustion in the room was palpable. Three years of fighting this tribunal. Three years of documenting their favouritism. And now, when we'd assembled the perfect rebuttal—five witnesses with contemporary documentation—they'd found a technical reason to exclude most of it.

"What do we do?" one lawyer asked.

I'd been thinking about that since reading the ruling. "We object. Formally. Under Article 32 of the UNCITRAL Rules, we object to the tribunal's non-compliance with the Rules."

I spent the weekend drafting that objection. It was thorough, detailed, and pointed. The tribunal's ruling constituted, in my view, a manifest disregard of the applicable rules, I wrote. It was a gross violation of Article 31(1), which required them to inquire whether we had further evidence before declaring the hearing closed.

They'd never inquired. They'd never declared the hearing closed. But now they were claiming it had been closed all along.

The objection went out on September 26.

* * * *

On September 29, the tribunal held another procedural meeting via ZOOM.

I attended with diminished expectations. The purpose of the meeting was to set dates for the post-hearing briefs and any remaining proceedings.

The tribunal announced that Wayne would be permitted to testify—but only in accordance with their September 23 ruling. Limited testimony. No additional witnesses. The hearing would take place on October 18.

They also set the schedule for post-hearing briefs:

November 28: Simultaneous submission of post-hearing briefs.

December 9: Simultaneous submission of post-hearing Reply briefs.

December 14: Final hearing for oral arguments.

I made notes, said little, and waited for the meeting to end.

Three weeks later, I would receive another ruling that would make even this limited hearing impossible.

* * * *

The email arrived on October 14, four days before Wayne was scheduled to testify.

The tribunal was cancelling the October 18 hearing.

I read the one-paragraph ruling twice, not quite believing what I was seeing.

They'd rejected four of our five witnesses. They'd limited the fifth to responding only to two paragraphs. And now they were cancelling even that limited hearing.

At the August 2022 evidentiary hearing, when the Company had ambushed us with John Doe's new evidence introduced without prior disclosure, the presiding arbitrator had made a clear determination. He'd reserved our right to respond. And he'd ruled that "the Company will bear the costs of any late submission."

The Company's counsel had accepted this condition on the record. "We accept that condition, sir."

That was the agreement. The Company created a need for rebuttal evidence through its procedural violation. They would pay the costs.

But the tribunal's September 23 ruling had reversed this. Now, the tribunal was demanding that both parties pay additional fees, split equally, as a condition for the October 18 hearing at which Wayne would testify.

At the September 27 procedural meeting, the Company's counsel had informed the tribunal that his client "may not be in a position to contribute towards this payment."

The Company—the party that had caused the need for additional hearings through their ambush, the party that had agreed to bear the costs—was now refusing to pay.

The presiding arbitrator's response was unequivocal: "If the fees are not paid, there would be no further hearing."

So the Company wouldn't pay. And if we didn't pay—if we didn't bear the costs for responding to their procedural violation—there would be no hearing at all.

The Company had created the need for this additional hearing. They had agreed to bear the costs. But now that they refused to pay, the tribunal threatened to cancel the hearing unless we paid instead.

On October 5, I sent a formal objection to the tribunal.

The ruling violated the agreement made on the record. More fundamentally, it violated Article 41(5) of the UNCITRAL Arbitration Rules, which governed the arbitration.

Article 41(5) was explicit: when a party challenges the tribunal's fee determination, the tribunal is required to proceed with the hearing during the process of challenge and review. The proceedings cannot be suspended simply because fees are disputed.

I had also written to the Company's counsel on October 6, requesting their cooperation to nominate an appointing authority to review the fee order. This was our right under Articles 41(3) and 41(4)(b) of the UNCITRAL Rules. The appointing authority would determine whether the fees were properly imposed.

Under the rules, the tribunal was required to continue the proceedings while that review took place.

But that's not what happened.

The tribunal's October 14 order stated: "The parties having failed to comply with the directive of the tribunal, the hearing date earlier fixed is hereby vacated."

It was a masterpiece of misdirection. "The parties" suggested mutual non-compliance. But the directive to pay had been imposed equally on both parties, even though only one—the Company—had necessitated additional hearings and had agreed to bear the costs. And when that party refused to pay, the tribunal cancelled the hearing entirely.

We hadn't "failed to comply." We had exercised our procedural right under Article 41 to challenge the fee determination and invoke the appointing authority mechanism. Under Article 41(5), the tribunal was required to proceed with the hearing during that challenge.

The tribunal knew this. Their own ruling acknowledged it: "The respondent's counsel informed the tribunal of its intention to formally oppose the ruling... The tribunal acknowledges that the respondent's counsel is at liberty to contest the ruling."

At liberty to contest—but apparently not at liberty to have the proceedings continue while that contest was resolved, as Article 41(5) explicitly required.

The October 14 ruling went on: "This directive is in compliance with the ruling of September 23, 2022. That ruling has not been successfully challenged."

But the challenge was pending. We had invoked the appointing authority review process. Under the UNCITRAL Rules, that meant the tribunal was required to proceed with the hearing rather than cancel it.

They'd accepted the Company's ambush at the hearing—new witness statements introduced without notice, twenty-five pages of testimony not disclosed in advance. But when we'd prepared a proper, comprehensive response through appropriate procedures, they'd first rejected it, then conditioned the limited response they'd approved on payment of fees that the Company had agreed to bear, and finally cancelled the hearing entirely when we challenged that fee determination.

And they'd done so in direct violation of Article 41(5) of the UNCITRAL Arbitration Rules.

The hearing wasn't rescheduled for Wayne's testimony. It was cancelled.

No witnesses. No rebuttal evidence. No cross-examination of John Doe on his new twenty-five pages of testimony.

I had written in my objection letter that the cancellation was "a constructive denial of fair hearing and equal treatment of the Respondent and a manifest disregard of the law and the rules."

Reading the tribunal's October 14 ruling, I saw no reason to revise that assessment.

The tribunal had systematically accommodated the Company's procedural violations while punishing us for following proper procedure. When the Company reneged on its agreement to bear the costs, the tribunal threatened to cancel the hearing unless we paid. And when we invoked the UNCITRAL Rules to challenge that determination, they cancelled the hearing in direct contravention of Article 41(5), which required them to proceed.

It was, as I noted in my activity log that day, precisely what it appeared to be: a tribunal that had decided the outcome and was now managing the procedure to reach it.

* * * *

I called the Special Assistant that afternoon.

"They cancelled it," I told him. "The hearing for Wayne. Just... cancelled. No alternative date."

There was silence on the line. Then: "Can they do that?"

"They just did. They've systematically blocked it. They've blocked every attempt we've made to respond to the Company's ambush. Four witnesses rejected outright. The fifth limited to two paragraphs. And now even that's cancelled."

"What's left?"

"The post-hearing brief. That's it. That's our last opportunity to present our case."

"The brief with your breakthrough argument? The staged contract theory?"

"Yes. Everything now depends on that brief. We can't call additional witnesses. We can't present rebuttal testimony. All we have left is the written submission."

"Can you win with just that?"

I thought about the Eureka argument. The staged contract structure. The legal theory that made the Company's three-billion-dollar claim impossible, regardless of any testimony.

"Yes," I said. "Because what we're going to put in that brief isn't dependent on witness testimony. It's based on the contract itself, the payment records, and their own documents. It's mathematical. Logical. Unassailable."

"You sound confident."

"I am. Because they can block our witnesses, cancel hearings, and manipulate procedures. But they can't change the contract's structure. They can't alter the payment records. They can't make the Company's claims add up when they mathematically don't."

After we hung up, I sat alone in my office as evening settled over Lagos.

My team was demoralised. We'd spent weeks assembling the perfect rebuttal—Wayne's powerful statement, four corroborating witnesses, and contemporary documentation. All of it excluded or cancelled.

But I wasn't demoralised. I was focused.

Because I'd known this might happen. I'd suspected the tribunal would find a way to block our rebuttal. That's why I'd held the eureka argument in reserve. That's why I hadn't deployed it at the hearing.

The tribunal's pattern of conduct had shown me something troubling: Taken cumulatively, the tribunal's interventions and procedural choices led me to believe they were no longer merely passive arbiters, but were engaging with the case in ways that consistently advantaged the Company. Questions that prompted witnesses. Suggestions about evidence. Characterisations that supported the Company's case.

The post-hearing brief was always going to be our knockout punch. The rebuttal witnesses would have been helpful, but they weren't essential. What was essential was the legal argument that proved the Company's claims were impossible.

And that argument was waiting, fully developed, ready to deploy.

* * * *

On October 17, I sent my final objection to the tribunal.

It was brief, professional, and pointed. The cancellation of the scheduled hearing was a non-compliance with the UNCITRAL Rules. The tribunal had offered us the right to respond, then systematically blocked every attempt to exercise that right.

I requested a certified true copy of their ruling. I requested a verbatim transcript of the September 29 procedural meeting.

I was building the record. Documenting every irregularity. Preserving evidence for whatever came after.

Because at this point, I had no illusions about this tribunal. At this point, I had serious concerns about the tribunal's lack of impartiality. The pattern of their procedural decisions, viewed cumulatively, appeared consistently unfavourable to us and favourable to the Company.

But I also had no doubt about the strength of our case. The settlement agreement was valid. The Company's own documents proved they hadn't performed. And the staged contract theory—the argument I would deploy in six weeks when the post-hearing brief was due—would make their three-billion-dollar claim mathematically impossible.

* * * *

That evening, I gathered my team in the conference room.

They looked exhausted. Defeated. Three years of work, and we'd just been blocked from presenting our strongest rebuttal evidence.

"I know this is discouraging," I said. "We put together a comprehensive response. Five witnesses. Contemporary documentation. Everything properly done. And the tribunal rejected it."

"So what do we do now?" one of them asked.

"Now we write the post-hearing brief. And we make it so strong, so clear, so unassailable that even this tribunal can't ignore it. They will find it very difficult to disregard."

"The staged contract argument?"

"Yes. That's our case now. Not witnesses, not testimony, not rebuttals. Just the pure legal theory backed by irrefutable documentary evidence."

"The brief will also address Wayne's documents," I said. "We'll explain what contemporaneous internal communications are, why they carry special evidentiary weight, and why Doe's failure to challenge them in 2015 was an acceptance of their truth. The tribunal may have blocked Wayne from testifying, but they can't block us from explaining the legal significance of documents already in the record."

"Will they understand the distinction?"

"They'll have to. Because we're going to cite the case law—English, Nigerian, international arbitration decisions—all saying the same thing: contemporaneous documents are the most reliable evidence. Wayne's emails and memos aren't just helpful to our case. They're the kind of evidence tribunals are supposed to give the greatest weight to."

The lawyer closest to me said, "You've been planning for this. This was always the strategy."

"I hoped we'd get to present the rebuttal," I admitted. "But I prepared for the possibility that we wouldn't. The eureka argument doesn't need Wayne or anyone else. Doesn't even need the hearing. It needs the contract, the payment records, the delivery records, and basic mathematics. All of which we have."

"And if the tribunal rules against us anyway?"

"Then we'll have documented three years of procedural concerns and decisions that raised questions about fair process. The Award will be vulnerable to challenge. But I don't think it will come to that. Because what we're going to show them in that brief isn't something they can dismiss or ignore. It's the truth, and it's undeniable."

I looked around the room at the three lawyers who'd fought beside me for three years. Who'd worked three hours every morning and three hours every evening for eight months analysing documents. Who'd endured a hostile tribunal, compromised procedures, and a pattern of decisions that consistently favoured the other side.

"Six weeks," I said. "We have six weeks to write the most important brief of our careers. The brief that saves the government three billion dollars. The brief that corners this tribunal so completely, they have no choice but to rule in our favour." The brief that presents evidence and articulates a legal argument so compelling that they will find it very difficult to rule against us."

"And then?"

"And then we wait. We wait for them to realise what we've done. We wait for them to understand that they've been outmanoeuvred. We wait for them to consider the arguments. We wait for their decision. We wait for the Award."

I smiled. "And we prepare for whatever comes after."

* * * *

November arrived. The deadline for the post-hearing brief was November 28—four weeks away.

I had my team organise everything we'd need: the complete contract, all payment records, the Company's own documents showing late deliveries and non-performance, the settlement agreement, and the timeline of events.

But mostly, I had the legal theory that had come to me in my bathroom on that Friday morning in late July.

The staged contract argument. The insight that changed everything.

Over the next four weeks, I would write the most important brief of my career. I would take that single insight and build it into an unassailable legal framework. I would use the Company's own evidence against them. I would show—mathematically, logically, irrefutably—that their three-billion-dollar claim was based on payment for work never performed.

And I would present it in a way that made the legal and factual conclusions inescapable. No room for different interpretation. A ruling against us would require disregarding the plain contractual terms and the undisputed documentary record.

The rebuttal witnesses had been blocked. The hearing had been cancelled. But the real fight had always been here, in the written brief, in the pure power of legal argument backed by irrefutable fact.

I opened a blank document on my laptop.

At the top, I typed: *Post-Hearing Brief - Federal Government of Nigeria*

Below that: *The Staged Contract Theory*

And then I began to write.

Chapter 10

When a decision-maker forms a view too early, the argument must be made so compelling that only one lawful outcome remains.

The Post-Hearing-Brief

November arrived with the clarity that comes after disappointment.

What follows reflects my professional assessment, based on the procedural record as it stood at the time, of how the post-hearing phase narrowed the tribunal's lawful decisional options.

The tribunal had rejected our rebuttal witnesses. They'd cancelled Wayne's testimony. They'd blocked every attempt we'd made to respond to the Company's ambush at the hearing. Over three years, a series of procedural accommodations—extensions, scheduling indulgences, and flexible application of procedural rules—consistently operated to the Company's advantage.

But none of that mattered now.

Because the real fight had never been about witnesses or testimony or oral arguments, the real fight was here, in the written brief. In the pure power of legal argument backed by irrefutable fact. The beauty of legal argument is that it doesn't depend on titles, accolades, or reputations. It depends on actual knowledge of the law—not perceived or imposed—but on a deep understanding of the law, the facts, strategy, and logical thinking, and these skills are not exclusive to any title, credential or designation.

And I had exactly what I needed.

The deadline for post-hearing briefs was November 28—four weeks away. The tribunal had ordered simultaneous submission, meaning both sides would file on the same day. Neither would see the other's brief beforehand. No opportunity to respond. No chance to adjust.

Which meant this brief had to be perfect. Complete. Unassailable.

The Discipline of Silence

Before I began building the structure, I needed to understand what I was really doing.

There is a temptation in advocacy—especially when facing a hostile or impatient tribunal, or one that appears to have formed preliminary views—to reveal everything as early as possible. To overwhelm resistance with brilliance. To force recognition through the sheer weight of argument.

I had resisted that temptation throughout the hearing.

The eureka argument—the staged contract theory that would dismantle the Company's entire claim—had never been fully articulated in the hearing room. Not because it was weak, but because it was structural. It didn't depend on witness credibility, demeanour, or cross-examination theatrics. It depended on arithmetic, chronology, and contractual logic.

And once articulated cleanly, it would leave no room to manoeuvre.

I had chosen not to deploy it orally. That decision was deliberate.

Oral hearings invite interruption. They invite premature judgment. They allow tribunals to redirect, reframe, or minimise points they find inconvenient. I'd watched it happen throughout our hearing—the presiding arbitrator's management of questioning, characterisation of the contract's structure, redirection of witnesses, and expressions of concern about time and detail.

A written brief, by contrast, speaks in full sentences. It cannot be cut off mid-thought. It must be read in its entirety, understood on its own terms. It must be answered—or evaded at the cost of intellectual coherence.

The tribunal could interrupt me in a hearing room. They could not interrupt 187 pages of tightly reasoned legal argument.

This was why the post-hearing brief mattered more than anything that had come before. This was my arena—the place where patience, precision, and preparation would overcome any preliminary views or predispositions.

The hearing had been a theatre. Necessary theatre, perhaps, but theatre nonetheless.

The brief would be mathematics.

The Structure

The post-hearing brief had to be comprehensive and detailed—not just our arguments, but the foundational legal principles underlying them.

This wasn't because the issues were complex. On the contrary, they were elementary. But the brief needed to be detailed for the sake of absolute clarity and completeness.

The tribunal's conduct throughout the proceedings—applying the Nigeria High Court procedure rules in an international arbitration conducted under the UNCITRAL Arbitration Rules, characterising procurement and a staged performance contract as a lease, waiving mandatory provisions of the rules, and making statements suggesting conclusions and findings of fact before hearing our defence—indicated that every principle needed to be articulated explicitly, with nothing left to inference or assumption.

So I built the brief from first principles.

What is a lease? Who owns the leftover equipment purchased with funds provided by one party? How are contracts formed—what is offer, acceptance, consideration? Whether acceptance of an offer can be inferred from the conduct of a party. The scope and application of constructive and resulting trusts.

These are foundational legal concepts—elementary concepts taught in first-year law school. But given what I'd observed, I could not rely on shared understanding. I had to ensure that every principle was explained thoroughly, every conclusion supported by detailed analysis, and every step of the reasoning made explicit.

The brief was structured to be completely self-contained and self-explanatory. Every legal conclusion was supported by careful analysis of the facts, the evidence and the law. Every principle was explained comprehensively. Every argument was developed fully, leaving nothing open to misunderstanding or misapplication.

It had to be a document that anyone—the tribunal, appellate courts, oversight bodies—could read and understand completely, without needing to make assumptions about how the law would be applied.

Clarity through completeness. Nothing left unexplained. Nothing left to chance.

The structure came first—three broad alternative defences, each one independently sufficient to defeat the Company's three-billion-dollar claim.

Defence One: Jurisdictional challenge. The Company lacked legal capacity because it had not been incorporated at the time the contract was signed. The Federal Government of Nigeria, as constituted in the contract and as named in the arbitration, wasn't a juristic person capable of entering into contracts or being pursued in arbitration.

This was a technical argument, legally sound but procedural. I didn't expect it to win. Tribunals rarely dismiss cases on jurisdictional grounds when three billion dollars is at stake. But it needed to be there. Complete. Documented. Sound law.

Defence Two: Mutual termination. The settlement agreement was valid, voluntary, and binding. Both parties had negotiated in good faith. The Company had expressed satisfaction—"it's all fair"—in writing. They'd sent a letter of appreciation. They'd received payment before signing. They'd complied with the settlement terms for ten months afterwards.

This defence was strong. We'd presented it powerfully at the hearing. The evidence was overwhelming.

But I anticipated the tribunal might find grounds to discount it, given the pattern of decisions over three years. I assumed that they wouldn't let a settlement agreement—however clear—stand in the way of a three-billion-dollar. Before this tribunal, a settlement agreement, however clear, might not be dispositive given the high stakes.

So, I needed something more. Something they couldn't escape. Something that made ruling against us impossible without destroying their own credibility.

Defence Three: The staged contract argument.

This was the eureka insight. The knockout punch. The argument that would be most difficult to dismiss.

And this was where I would spend most of my time.

The Staged Contract Theory

I began with the fundamentals. What was this contract, structurally?

The Fireforce Agreement wasn't a simple purchase or performance contract. It wasn't a lease. It was a staged procurement and performance contract with specific timelines, deliverables, and milestone payments.

Stage One: Equipment procurement. The government would pay approximately US$30 million immediately after signing. The Company would use those funds to procure all the military hardware—weapons, ammunition, armoured vehicles, attack and transport helicopters, and equipment. Some were to be purchased. Some were to be leased. Timeline: 14 to 21 days.

Stages Two through Five: Operations. Once the equipment was delivered and positioned, the government would make subsequent payments. These were lease rental fees for the leased and deployed equipment, as well as ongoing personnel and supply costs—timeline: Monthly payments over the six-month operation.

The structure was clear. The government provided all the procurement funding up front. The Company would deliver the equipment quickly. Then the operation would commence, and the government would pay for the equipment's use over time.

But what happened if the Company didn't deliver the equipment within the agreed-upon timelines?

What happened if Stage One wasn't completed before Stage Two payments came due?

What happened if the contract was terminated before the later stages were performed?

The answer was simple: those later-stage payments weren't due. They hadn't been earned. The purpose for which they were intended—lease rental fees for deployed equipment—hadn't been achieved.

You can't claim rent for equipment you never delivered.

* * * *

Twenty-five months later, the tribunal would adopt this analysis in its entirety.

They would call the contract "STAGED"—use the exact word, in capital letters, as if it were obvious. They would write: "Multiple phases contingent on delivery and performance."

They would accept our compartmentalisation structure—Category A, Category B, Category C, D, E. They would agree: "The availability of the assets (weapons and ammunition) became the benchmark by which milestone payments were made."

And they would conclude exactly what I was writing: "If it fails to perform its supply obligation in Category A, it will not be entitled to payment in Category B."

The Company's three-billion-dollar claim would be dismissed in its entirety. Not one dollar awarded.

But I didn't know that yet. I was writing blind, building an argument I believed was unassailable, hoping it would be enough.

* * * *

At this point, the contract structure could be explained in simpler terms.

Consider this: you engage a contractor to dig a borehole within five days, install a submersible pump within two days thereafter, and construct an overhead tank within ten days. Payment is staged—first for the borehole, then for the pump, then for the tank.

If the borehole is not completed within the agreed time, would payment for the pump be due? Of course not. The pump cannot be installed without the borehole. The obligation to pay for later stages depends on the completion of earlier ones.

And if the need for the borehole is time-sensitive—if circumstances change and the project is abandoned before completion—no rational system of contract law would require payment for stages that were never performed.

The same logic applies here. The Company sought payment for later contractual stages despite failing to complete the foundational stage within the stipulated timelines. The claim was, in effect, for pumps and tanks where the borehole had never been dug.

Stage Two: The Proof

I analysed the Stage Two payment in detail—six categories, each examined against the Company's own evidence.

Manpower costs? Already paid for three months under Stage One. The subcontractor had testified they'd been paid in full, three months in advance. The next manpower payment wasn't due until those three months had expired.

Vehicle lease payments? The vehicles hadn't arrived. Their own delivery certificate showed arrival on March 24, 2015—more than three months late. How could lease payments be due for vehicles that hadn't been delivered?

Helicopter lease payments? Same problem. Their air waybills showed helicopters still being shipped in late January 2015. The lease payments scheduled for December 17, 2014, couldn't be owed for helicopters that wouldn't arrive for another six weeks.

Night vision equipment, communication gear, and a surgical unit? No proof of delivery by the scheduled payment date. Their own documents—the air waybills they'd submitted—showed these items still in transit weeks after the payment was supposedly due.

I went through each category systematically, using their evidence against them. Every air waybill. Every invoice. Every delivery certificate. All of it is proving to be late delivery or non-delivery.

The analysis was devastating because it used the Company's own documents to prove they hadn't performed. They'd documented their own failure.

For Stages Three, Four, and Five, the same principle applied. Each payment depended on prior stages being completed and equipment being delivered. The contract explicitly required proof that "all manpower, vehicles and air assets as described in the contract have been delivered to Nigeria" before the Stage payment could be made.

Those proofs were never provided. It couldn't be provided—because the equipment hadn't arrived on schedule.

Without proof, no payment was due.

"Subject to Regulatory Approval"

I knew the Company would hide behind one phrase buried in the contract: "subject to regulatory approval."

At the hearing, whenever I'd pressed the Company's star witness about why equipment hadn't arrived within the stipulated timelines, he'd gestured vaguely toward regulatory complications. Import approvals. Government clearances. Bureaucratic delays are beyond their control.

But "subject to regulatory approval" is a conditional provision. It doesn't eliminate the time requirement—it suspends performance only while regulatory approval is pending.

The burden of proof sits squarely on the party claiming the suspension.

To invoke this provision successfully, the Company would need to demonstrate three things: First, that regulatory approval was actually required. Second, they applied for such approval promptly after contract signing. Third, the approval process itself caused delays, preventing them from meeting the contractual deadlines.

They had provided no such proof.

At the hearing, I'd asked their witness repeatedly for documentation of regulatory delays. Applications for import permits. Communications with Nigerian authorities. Evidence that they'd been prevented from timely delivery by government bureaucracy.

He'd provided nothing specific. Just vague assertions that "these things take time."

The Company wasn't some naive first-time contractor. They were a sophisticated international private military company. They'd worked in multiple African countries. They'd arranged weapons shipments across borders before. They knew—or should have known—about regulatory requirements when they drafted the contract.

And they had drafted it. Every word. Including those timelines. They'd assigned the procurement responsibility to themselves. They'd set the deadlines without consulting us.

They couldn't now claim surprise that regulatory approvals were required.

The timelines weren't incidental terms. They were the essence of the bargain. Why had the government chosen this Company? Speed. The promise of rapid deployment. Equipment delivered in fourteen days, twenty-one days, not months or years.

The phrase "subject to regulatory approval" didn't protect them—it required them to prove delays. They had no proof.

Which meant the timelines stood. The Company had breached. And the payments conditioned on timely performance weren't due.

Constructive Trust Argument

But there was another dimension to the equipment dispute that needed to be addressed. Even if—hypothetically—the Company had delivered everything on time and performed flawlessly, they still couldn't claim ownership of the leftover equipment or its monetary value.

Because of a principle of equity that trumped whatever the contract said or didn't say: constructive trust.

The Company's position throughout had been that all equipment belonged to them. They relied on a statement buried in the contract's appendix—the equipment is supplied on a lease basis. Latching onto this provision, they'd characterised the contract as a "lease"—the government was supposedly leasing weapons, vehicles, and helicopters from the Company. Therefore, at contract termination, everything should revert to them or be paid for.

The tribunal had accepted this characterisation. During the hearing, the presiding arbitrator stated openly—without hearing our defence or engaging in contract interpretation—that "the equipment is purchased, and then leased to the Nigerian army." A conclusion that doesn't make sense and isn't stated in the contract. How does a government provide funds to a contractor to purchase weapons, lease them from the contractor, and then hand them back to the contractor for a covert operation? This is what the Company argued, and the tribunal accepted without even hearing from us.

It was a premature conclusion, influenced by the Company's framing rather than the contract's actual structure.

But even setting aside whether the contract was truly a lease which it wasn't—there was a fundamental problem with the Company's ownership claim: they hadn't paid for any of it.

Every dollar spent on procurement came from the government. The Company contributed nothing. They were simply the intermediary through which government funds flowed to purchase or lease equipment for a specific purpose: the military operation.

Under Nigerian law—and equity principles recognised across common law jurisdictions—when Party A provides all the funds to Party B to procure property for a specific purpose, Party B holds that property in trust for Party A, regardless of whose name appears on purchase documents.

This is the constructive trust doctrine.

I found the case law readily. In *Huebner v. A.I.E. & P.M. Co Ltd.*, the Supreme Court of Nigeria clearly articulated the principle: "Constructive trust is imposed by equity regardless of the intention of the parties."

The court had explained further: "A constructive trust is neither granted nor accepted—it is foisted upon the parties by the operation of law."

And most importantly: "A constructive trust is the formula through which the conscience of equity finds expression."

The application to our case was straightforward:

The government had provided approximately US$30 million in the first stage payment specifically for equipment procurement. The contract explicitly stated this: the payment was made "to secure" the items listed in Schedule 1.

The Company used those funds to purchase weapons, ammunition, and other equipment. Some were delivered. Some weren't. Some were used during the operation. Some remained.

Under the constructive trust doctrine, all equipment purchased with government funds—regardless of whether it was delivered, used, or left over—belonged beneficially to the government. The Company held legal title only as trustee.

This wasn't about contract interpretation. This wasn't about what the parties intended. This was equity imposing an outcome based on fundamental fairness: you can't use someone else's money to buy property and then claim it as your own.

I wrote this section of the brief with particular care:

The Claimant holds the residue of all equipment purchased with the funds of the Respondent as both a resulting trustee and as a constructive trustee for the Respondent. A constructive trust is foisted upon the parties by the operation of law. It is the formula through which the conscience of equity finds expression.

So long as there is no contractual transfer of the residue of equipment purchased with the Respondent's funds, equity deems them as that of the Respondent.

The beauty of this argument was its inevitability. The Company could dispute contract interpretation. They could argue about delivery dates and performance obligations. But they couldn't dispute the source of the funds.

Every bank record, every wire transfer, every payment receipt showed the same thing: government money funding equipment procurement.

And there was a precedent even more directly on point. *In Re Pedro*, a Nigerian court had addressed exactly this situation. When property is provided for a specific purpose using funds from a particular source, and that purpose is completed or abandoned, who owns what's left?

The court held that the party providing the funds held beneficial ownership through resulting or constructive trust.

I included both cases in the brief with full citations and relevant excerpts. Then I addressed the practical implications:

If the Company wanted to claim the leftover equipment, they would need to show they had a contractual right to it. The contract was silent on this—paragraph 10 of Schedule 1 mentioned "supplied equipment" being offered for sale or repatriation, but said nothing about purchased equipment.

That silence, under the *contra proferentem* rule of contract interpretation—the principle that ambiguous contract terms should be interpreted against the party that drafted them—should be construed against the Company as the drafter of the contract.

And even if the contract had explicitly given them ownership—which it didn't—equity could override that explicit provision if allowing it would produce an unconscionable result.

Taking equipment purchased entirely with someone else's money while serving merely as a procurement agent would be unconscionable.

I sat back after writing this section and considered what it meant for the tribunal.

We'd now closed off multiple lines of argument:

The staged contract theory proved that the later payments weren't due because the equipment hadn't been delivered and the stages hadn't been performed.

The constructive trust doctrine proved that even if everything had been delivered and performed perfectly, the leftover equipment still belonged to the government, not the Company.

The settlement agreement proved that the parties had already resolved and terminated their obligations by mutual consent.

The tribunal would have to reject basic contract law, fundamental equity principles, and clear documentary evidence to rule in favour of the Company.

They'd have to craft an Award explaining why someone could claim ownership of property purchased entirely with someone else's money.

They'd have to explain why payments were due for work that was never performed and equipment that was never delivered.

They'd have to explain why a settlement agreement, voluntarily signed after negotiation with expressions of satisfaction, somehow didn't mean what it clearly said.

Every avenue of escape was blocked.

The constructive trust argument was particularly satisfying because it addressed what had troubled me during the hearing—the presiding arbitrator's casual acceptance of the "lease" characterisation without examining whether it made any sense.

He'd said the equipment was "purchased and then leased to the Nigerian army" as if this were obvious and uncontroversial.

But it wasn't obvious. It was illogical. And now I've shown why: even if that's what happened, which it didn't—the purchaser using someone else's funds holds the property in trust for the funder.

This is an elementary principle of the law of equity. First-year law school material. But apparently it needed to be spelt out to a tribunal composed entirely of senior lawyers that had spent three years accepting the Company's characterisations without scrutiny.

I added a final paragraph to this section:

The Claimant cannot claim monetary value for equipment it holds in trust for the Respondent. To do so would be to profit from its position as trustee—a fundamental breach of fiduciary duty that equity will not permit.

There. The argument was complete. Unassailable. Supported by Supreme Court authority.

If the tribunal wanted to give the Company three billion dollars now, they'd have to explain why Nigerian equity law didn't apply. Why constructive trusts—recognised for centuries in common law—somehow didn't exist in this case.

I sent this section to my team with a note: "This closes the ownership argument completely. They can't claim the equipment, and they can't claim its value. The trust doctrine makes both impossible."

One of them replied within an hour: "This is elegant. You've made it impossible for them to rule for the Company without ignoring fundamental legal principles that every first-year law student would recognise."

"Exactly," I wrote back. "That's the point. Ruling against us would require disregarding fundamental legal principles. Every argument in this brief is designed to make ruling against us professionally embarrassing for them."

The constructive trust section reinforced the broader legal framework. Ruling for the Company would require disregarding well-established equity principles.

And I believed the strength of the legal argument would ultimately prevail.

Writing for the Record

As I continued writing, I began to understand something more fundamental about what I was doing.

I was not writing to persuade the tribunal. I was writing for the record.

My audience was not the three arbitrators who had interrupted, reprimanded, mischaracterised the contract structure, pre-judged the case and signalled impatience throughout the hearing. My audience was the Award itself.

An arbitral Award must explain itself. It must reconcile the facts, the law, and the outcome. It must withstand scrutiny—by courts, by historians, by conscience. And, crucially, in explaining why it ruled the way it did, it must address the arguments made.

I structured the brief so that any Award granting the Company relief would have to ignore the staged nature of the contract, disregard undisputed payment records, contradict the settlement agreement, and justify billions for non-delivery and non-performance.

In other words, it would have to confess its own incoherence.

Every section I wrote was built toward that inevitability. Not through accusation or outrage, but through structure. Chronology. Tables. Plain language. The kind of methodical, step-by-step analysis that left no gaps, no ambiguities, no room for convenient misinterpretation.

If the tribunal wanted to rule for the Company, they would have to explain—in writing, for the permanent record—why money paid for undelivered weapons had magically transformed into a three-billion-dollar entitlement. They would have to explain why the lease rental fees were due for equipment that never arrived. They would have to explain why payments were owed for stages the Company had never performed.

* * * *

The tribunal would, in fact, adopt our record.

They would find the Company committed "continuing breach." They would confirm Nigeria overpaid by nearly three million dollars. They would create a detailed table—forty items from the Company's own documents—showing not one delivered on time.

They would reject every excuse the Company offered. Regulatory approval claims: rejected. Christmas delays: rejected. Time is not fundamental: rejected.

They would vindicate our case completely.

But they would take twenty-five months to write it. Twenty-five months after announcing they had "a position." Because, as I suspected, they would spend those months looking for an escape route that didn't exist.

And in explaining all of that, they would have to reveal themselves.

* * * *

There were things I deliberately did not include.

I did not dwell on the alleged attempted bribery of the government's star witness. There had been other improper approaches during the life of the case—to me, to my team—that I had chosen not to memorialise in the brief. Not because they were insignificant, but because responding to them would have turned the case into something else entirely. My brief was about the law and the evidence. Cataloguing corruption allegations would have been a distraction—and would have dignified tactics that deserved no response.

I did not accuse the tribunal of corruption or collusion. I did not speculate on motive. I did not question their integrity, choosing instead to focus on the legal and factual record.

Everything I wrote was anchored in the record—in facts so undisputed that denial would have been embarrassing.

That restraint was not timidity. It was confidence.

The stronger the argument, the less noise it requires. Accusations can be dismissed as bitterness. Speculation can be ignored as paranoia. But mathematics cannot be argued with. Contract language cannot be wished away. Payment records cannot be altered retroactively.

The strength of the argument would be measured against professional standards. I was cornering them with their own professional reputations.

The three arbitrators were Senior Advocates of Nigeria—a title accorded to senior trial lawyers who have achieved distinction in their practice. They had presented themselves throughout the hearing as competent and knowledgeable. They would want the Award to reflect that professional image.

But ruling for the Company despite the evidence would be difficult to reconcile with professional standing.

Anybody reading an Award that ignored the staged contract structure, dismissed contemporaneous payment records, and granted monetary claims for unperformed work would question the reasoning—would immediately understand what had happened. Not a mistake. Not a difference of opinion. Something worse.

Any legally trained reader of the record would understand this. The tribunal understood this too. Or they would, once they read the brief.

Which meant they had two options: rule in our favour, or abandon the case entirely.

And abandoning the case would be even more damaging to their reputations than ruling against the Company.

So they would rule for us. Eventually. After spending months trying to find an escape route that didn't exist.

That was the real power of what I'd written. Not just persuasion. Strategic positioning.

The Final Push

By mid-November, I had completed the core argument—approximately 150 pages analysing the staged structure, demonstrating non-performance, proving that payments weren't due.

I sent sections to my team as I completed them. They'd review, suggest refinements, and catch any weaknesses.

After I finished the Stage Two analysis, one of them called. "This is devastating. You're using their own delivery records to prove they didn't deliver on time. Their own documents destroy their claim."

"That's the point," I said. "Every air waybill they submitted, every invoice, every certificate—it all proves late delivery. They documented their own failure."

"The tribunal can't ignore this."

"I imagine they'll try. But we're not giving them any room. By the time they finish reading this, they'll understand that the Company is claiming payment for work that was never performed."

"How long do you think the Award will take?"

I'd been thinking about that. The pattern of decisions over three years had consistently favoured the Company. But this brief would make that impossible.

"Twelve months minimum," I said. "Maybe longer. Because they're going to see the strength of the argument. Ruling for the Company would be very difficult to justify, given the evidence. But ruling in our favour means accepting an analysis that makes their earlier conduct harder to explain. They're going to spend months trying to find a way out."

They would take twenty-five months—more than twice my estimate. Not because the case was complex—the Award would call it straightforward. But because, in my assessment, they were doing exactly what I predicted: searching for an escape route that professional standards wouldn't allow.

"And if they can't find a way out?"

"Then they'll have no choice. They'll rule in our favour. Because the strength of the legal argument will be difficult to dismiss."

* * * *

On November 20, eight days before the deadline, I had a complete draft. One hundred and eighty-seven pages.

I sent it to my team with a note: *Review quickly but carefully. This is what wins the case. When they read this, they'll understand they have no escape.*

Over the next few days, comments came back. Suggestions for clarity. Requests to expand certain sections. Questions about case citations.

We refined it together. Tightened the language. Strengthened the weakest points. Made the strong points unassailable.

By November 26, it was ready.

I read through the entire brief one final time. From the summary at the beginning—laying out the three alternative defences—through the detailed stage-by-stage analysis, to the conclusion.

The conclusion was simple:

The Claimant is not entitled to payment for Stages Two through Five because those stages were never performed. The equipment was not delivered within the timelines specified. The operations contemplated by those stage payments never occurred. The contract was terminated before those stages could begin.

The Claimant cannot claim three billion dollars for work it never did, for equipment it never delivered, for operations that never happened.

The claim should be dismissed in its entirety.

I closed the document and sat back.

It was done.

One hundred and eighty-seven pages that would constrain even a hostile tribunal to rule in our favour. Because ruling against us would require them to ignore basic mathematics, contradict their own case law, and accept the logical impossibility that someone could be paid for work they'd never performed.

We'd cornered them completely—the brief constrained the range of legally defensible outcomes.

* * * *

On November 28, the Company's counsel, the tribunal secretary, and I coordinated by email to ensure simultaneous submission. We confirmed readiness, agreed on the exact time, and at 11:47 a.m., both counsel hit send together.

My email went to all three arbitrators and the Company's counsel. Subject line: Respondent's Post-Hearing Brief - Simultaneous Submission.

Attached: 187 pages.

My team gathered in my office that afternoon. We'd been working toward this moment for three years. Through three years of procedural obstacles and concerning tribunal conduct, we'd built a defence that couldn't be ignored.

"They'll take months to respond," I said. "Maybe a year. Because they're going to realise what we've done, we haven't just presented a strong argument. We've trapped them with their own professional reputations."

"How?" one of them asked.

"They're Senior Advocates. They've carried themselves throughout this case as experienced, competent professionals. Now they have to choose: rule in our favour, or issue an Award that challenges their standing."

"From the conduct of the proceedings and pattern of rulings thus far, it appeared they wanted to rule for the Company."

"Yes. But now they can't. Because if they ignore the arguments in this brief—arguments based on basic contract principles, simple mathematics, and the Company's own evidence—they'll challenge their reputations. Every lawyer who reads that Award will know what happened."

The lawyer who'd become closest to me said, "You think they'll rule for us?"

"I think they have two options: rule in our favour or abandon the case entirely. And abandoning the case would be even worse for their reputations. So yes, they'll rule for us. Eventually. After they've spent months trying to find an escape that doesn't exist."

"How long?"

"Twelve months minimum. Probably longer."

He smiled. "You sound very certain."

"I am certain. Because I've read that brief probably fifty times. And every time, I see the same thing: there's no escape. They're cornered."

The Closing Arguments Dispute

The Company's brief arrived the same day, part of the simultaneous submission. I read through it that evening.

It was exactly what I'd expected. They restated their claims. They argued they'd performed substantially. They claimed the settlement was obtained through duress. They asserted their claim for three billion dollars, including interest and costs. No depth. No serious legal argument. Didn't debunk any of the legal issues we raised. Their presentation demonstrated a complete misunderstanding of the contract's structure and what was required for their case to succeed.

They hadn't addressed the staged contract argument. They couldn't have—they didn't know we'd developed it. We'd held it in reserve specifically for this moment.

Their entire brief assumed the tribunal would accept their characterisation of the contract as a lease agreement. But we'd demonstrated it wasn't a lease. It was a staged procurement and performance contract with specific timelines and deliverables.

Once you correctly understood the structure, their claims collapsed.

* * * *

Then, on December 26, two days after Christmas, I received an unexpected email from the tribunal's secretary.

The tribunal was scheduling a hearing for "adoption of final addresses"—oral closing arguments—proposed dates: January 23 or 24, 2023.

I stared at the email for a long moment. I was on vacation thousands of miles away and didn't bother to respond.

This wasn't in the procedural rules. The UNCITRAL Arbitration Rules didn't require oral closing arguments after written submissions. We'd already exchanged post-hearing briefs and reply briefs. What more was there to say? The tribunal refused to allow our rebuttal because, in their view, "the hearings had closed."

I imagined and indeed believed this to be another accommodation, allowing the Company to adjust, to respond to arguments they hadn't anticipated.

On December 28, I replied politely, noting that I was travelling and requesting that if the purpose was solely to adopt briefs, parties be allowed to do so by email.

The tribunal insisted: "The adoption of final written submissions is an integral part of the instant proceedings."

I discussed it with my team. "They want oral arguments. After we've already submitted comprehensive written briefs."

"Why?"

"Because they've read our brief. They understand they're trapped. Now they want us to argue orally, hoping we'll say something that gives them an opening."

On January 4, 2023, I sent my response to the tribunal. The tone was measured but firm. I pointed out that the adoption of written addresses wasn't part of arbitral jurisprudence. The UNCITRAL Rules made no provision for it.

I concluded: *We believe the tribunal has enough materials before it to resolve the dispute. We therefore urge the tribunal to proceed to hand down the Award.*

The presiding arbitrator responded on January 18, explaining that closing arguments were "a uniquely significant procedure in the English common law system."

But this was not a judicial proceeding—it was a practical arbitration proceeding that followed specific rules. The statement "a uniquely significant procedure in the English common law system" came across as if the proceedings were a mock trial.

On January 24, I replied again: *The tribunal now refers to oral closing arguments, no longer the adoption of final written addresses. The applicable rule made no provision for closing arguments. The tribunal's insistence on conducting the arbitration as if it were a proceeding before a municipal court amount to litigization of arbitration.*

I couldn't resist adding: *The same tribunal that refused to accept crucial rebuttal evidence on the wrong ground that the hearing had closed now wants to conduct further hearings that the parties are not interested in, without charge. What is most important to an Arbitral Tribunal is factual evidence, not sophistry.*

The tribunal went silent for a week.

Then, on February 3, the secretary sent a brief email:

The tribunal has given the matter deep and mature consideration and elects to proceed to deliver an Award. The tribunal hereby waives the procedural order compelling parties to adopt their written address.

I forwarded the email to my team with a single line: *They backed down. Now we wait for the Award.*

* * * *

The wait would be long. Twenty-five months from the date they foreclosed the Company's post-hearing reply brief to the date they delivered the Award.

But when it came, it would vindicate everything. The staged contract framework—adopted word-for-word. The Company's failures—documented in the tribunal's own table. The three-billion-dollar claim—dismissed entirely.

One hundred eighty-seven pages of argument. Twenty-five months of deliberation. Complete victory.

The brief had done exactly what I designed it to do: make ruling against us professionally impossible.

Chapter 11

The 25-Month Wait

This chapter recounts events as they unfolded on the procedural record and reflects my professional assessment, based on timing, sequence, and outcomes, rather than any claim of knowledge of internal deliberations or motives.

The hearing had ended on August 9, 2022.

At the hearing, during the cross-examination of the Company's witness before I opened our defence, the presiding arbitrator had made a remarkable statement:

"Quite honestly, we have a full picture of what may have happened. So why don't we limit it to what may need explanation from his cross-examination? Quite honestly, most of what you are asking up to now, of course, we sat here, and we have our position as we listen."

We have a full picture. We have our position.

They had announced—in open hearing, on the record—that they had already formed a view of the case. This occurred before hearing the Respondent's defence—before reviewing our evidence, and before considering our post-hearing submissions or legal argument.

On its face, the statement conveyed that the tribunal had reached a settled, or at least an operative, view of the dispute at a stage when the Respondent had not yet been heard. Whether that was the tribunal's intention or not, the timing and wording of the statement raised concerns about procedural sequencing and the appearance of impartiality. The statement was not inferred or reconstructed; it was captured verbatim in the hearing transcript.

How did the arbitrators form their opinion, on what facts? If the arbitrators could form their opinion on the case based on the facts presented by the Company only, why was the hearing necessary?

If they already had "their position" in August 2022, why did it take them twenty-five months to issue the Award?

That question would define the longest Wait of my professional life.

* * * *

We submitted our post-hearing brief on November 28, 2022. One hundred and eighty-seven pages that dismantled the Company's claims with mathematical precision. The staged contract theory. The constructive trust doctrine. The settlement agreement evidence. Every escape route blocked. Every counterargument anticipated.

The Company submitted its post-hearing brief on the same day we did—November 28, 2022. Both parties then had until 6 p.m. on December 9 to submit post-hearing reply briefs.

We were ready. They were not.

On December 9, before 6 p.m., I informed the tribunal, with a copy to all parties, including the Company's counsel, that our reply brief was prepared and ready for simultaneous exchange. The Secretary responded that the Company's counsel had informed him he couldn't submit as agreed—he was in transit. He would be ready on Monday, December 12.

Monday arrived. I wrote to the tribunal seeking confirmation that we could proceed with the simultaneous exchange. The Secretary replied that the Company's counsel was now bereaved and would submit at noon on Tuesday, December 13.

Tuesday came. By 5:14 p.m., there was still no word from the Company's counsel.

This was the same pattern I'd been documenting for three years. Missed deadlines. Vague excuses. The tribunal accommodating every Delay.

But this time, I'd had enough.

I wrote to the tribunal. The email was direct, perhaps more so than any communication I'd sent before. I pointed out the pattern: the Company had taken about six months to submit their statement of claim, twelve months to submit their reply to our defence, and had submitted incomplete documents that the tribunal had to accommodate. Now they were treating the post-hearing reply brief deadline with the same casual disregard.

I requested that the tribunal foreclose the Company from filing its reply brief. They'd had the same deadline as us. They'd agreed to a simultaneous exchange. They'd failed to comply—again.

On December 15, 2022, the tribunal issued an order.

For the first time in three years, they imposed consequences on the Company:

- A cost of US$3,000 against the Company and their counsel, to be paid regardless of the final outcome.
- The Company was foreclosed from filing a post-hearing reply brief
- We were ordered to submit our reply within 24 hours

That same day, I submitted our reply brief—the one we'd prepared by December 9, ready and waiting.

The tribunal acknowledged receipt.

For the first time in this arbitration, the Company had missed a deadline and actually faced consequences. No extension. No accommodation. Just enforcement of the rules. That's the way it ought to be. That is the way serious arbitrators conduct arbitrations. Otherwise, arbitration loses its essence. This arbitration could've been concluded in nine months or less if the tribunal had followed this path.

I suspected the real reason: the Company's counsel had been overwhelmed by our 187-page post-hearing brief and couldn't respond. The staged contract theory, the constructive trust doctrine, the settlement agreement evidence, the detailed legal analysis, the comprehensive dismantling of their claims—it was unanswerable.

And now they wouldn't get the chance to try.

By mid-December 2022, the evidential record was complete. The tribunal had everything they needed. There were no outstanding procedural issues.

The median length of an arbitration is between ten and sixteen months. A typical arbitration Award takes three months after final submissions. Complex cases might take slightly longer. But there was nothing procedurally complicated about what remained. There was nothing complicated about the claim, the contract, or the issues in controversy. The tribunal simply needed to evaluate the evidence, apply the law, and write its decision.

December passed. Then January. February. March.

My team would ask periodically: "Any word from the tribunal?"

"Not yet."

"How much longer?"

"As long as it takes."

By June 2023—six months after the briefs—one of my senior lawyers raised it more directly.

"This is taking a long time."

"Yes."

They said at the hearing that they already had their position. That was ten months ago. What's the Delay?

I'd been thinking about that question since December. "They read our brief. And they realised their position—the one they'd formed before hearing our defence—was impossible to justify in writing."

"So they're reconsidering?"

"They're looking for an escape route. Some way to rule for the Company without it being very difficult to justify. But they won't find one."

"You sound certain."

"I am certain. Because I wrote that brief knowing exactly what it would do to them. Every argument was designed to be very difficult to dismiss given professional standards. They either rule for us, or they issue an Award that would be very difficult to justify."

"And if they just... never issue an Award?"

"Then their reputations suffer even more. Arbitrators who accept fees and then abandon cases? That's worse than issuing a bad Award. They're stuck. Eventually, they'll accept that and issue the ruling we both know is inevitable."

* * * *

Six months became twelve. Twelve became eighteen.

What follows is included not as fact, but as unverified information conveyed to me by a third party during the period of delay. I did not rely on this information in any submission, did not investigate it independently, and express no conclusion as to its accuracy. I recount it solely to explain questions that arose at the time regarding the arbitration's extended timeline.

Information reached me during this period that may explain some of what had happened earlier in the case.

In March 2023, the ATTEP contact called again. This time, with claims about why the Company had taken eighteen months to file its statement of claim and Reply.

"You know it took them forever to file their case, right?" he said. "Extensions after extensions."

"Yes. The rules gave them forty-five days total. They took about eighteen months in total."

"There was a reason," he said. "The Company's principal became entangled, during that period, in unrelated matters that significantly disrupted his availability and operations."

He referred to alleged external investigations involving individuals associated with the Company and to circumstances that, in his account, delayed the prosecution of the arbitration. He did not allege misconduct by the Company in the arbitration itself, and I make no such allegation here.

I had no independent means of verifying these claims. I therefore treat them only as contextual information offered to explain the timing of certain procedural delays, not as established fact.

I wrote this down carefully. "When was this?"

"2019, 2020. Maybe a bit earlier." He referred, in general terms, to serious external allegations involving persons connected to the Company, unrelated to the arbitration. I did not verify these claims and express no view on their accuracy. I note them only because of their asserted temporal coincidence with procedural delays in the case.

"How long was he on the wanted list?"

"The delay lasted exactly as long as necessary." According to the contact, some of Sweeny's personnel were arrested, prosecuted, convicted, and sentenced. He claimed that only after that criminal case was completely closed did the arbitration proceed to the hearing.

This information from this contact was concerning. And I didn't know what to make of it.

I had no way to verify these claims independently. But after that call, I examined the arbitration timeline.

The pattern was notable: several extensions without justification. The hearing wasn't scheduled until 2022—after the timeframe the contact had described for the alleged criminal proceedings.

Whether there was any actual connection between these events, I couldn't say with certainty. But the timing raised questions I couldn't ignore.

* * * *

By July 2024—nineteen months after we'd submitted the post-hearing reply brief—the tribunal sent an unexpected email.

They wanted clarification on a specific point in our post-hearing brief. A reference I'd made to certain payment records and breach of confidentiality. Could I provide additional detail?

I read the email twice. After nineteen months of silence, they were asking about a minor evidentiary detail.

Which meant they were working on the Award. They'd read our brief carefully enough to identify specific references that needed explanation. They were building their analysis, trying to construct reasoning that would withstand scrutiny. I thought this was a good sign.

I responded professionally, providing the requested information. But I also added:

"The Respondent notes that more than nineteen months have passed since the submission of post-hearing briefs. This delay is extraordinary and concerning. The Respondent respectfully requests that the tribunal proceed expeditiously to issue its Award."

That letter—expressing concern about the delay—would later become the basis for the disciplinary summons against me. The tribunal would claim I'd imputed improper motives and attacked their integrity.

But in July 2024, I simply needed them to understand: we were waiting. The delay was unjustifiable. And they needed to issue the

Award.

The Inevitable Outcome

By September 2024—twenty-five months after the end of the evidentiary hearing—they'd exhausted every option.

They couldn't find a way to rule against us. They couldn't find a middle ground that made legal sense. They couldn't abandon the case without even worse reputational damage.

The procedural and legal posture of the case had narrowed the range of defensible outcomes.

In my professional assessment, an Award against the Respondent would have required disregarding core findings ultimately accepted by the tribunal itself.

They had only one defensible choice left: to rule in our favour.

But that choice came with consequences for me.

I'd checked industry statistics while waiting. Median arbitrations—from notice to final—take 10 to 16 months. Post-hearing to Award typically takes three to six months.

Ours took twenty-five months just for the Award—more than four times the normal timeframe for what the tribunal itself would call a straightforward case.

They'd announced their position in August 2022. They'd received our unanswerable brief in November 2022.

And they'd spent twenty-five months looking for an escape route that didn't exist.

September 6, 2024.

The email arrived at 2:47 p.m.—the moment I described at the beginning of this book.

"Final Award - *[REDACTED] v. Federal Government of Nigeria.*"

Five years. Three billion dollars. Twenty-five months of waiting.

I screamed. I've told you about that scream. About the raw emotion. About calling my team, my wife, about the international investors who'd happened to be in my office.

What I haven't told you is what I did next.

I went home to read what the tribunal had written. To understand how they'd ruled. To see whether they'd addressed the pre-judgment. To learn whether twenty-five months had changed anything.

To discover what victory looked like when those in power write the official account.

Chapter 12

The Award

I opened the email. The Award attached—Ninety-one pages—and began reading systematically.

What the tribunal Found

The Company had claimed approximately three billion dollars. The sum included the monetary value of equipment they said belonged to them, pre-award interest from the inception of their alleged obligation, and post-award interest until "full liquidation."

Three billion dollars.

The tribunal awarded them nothing.

Not one dollar of the principal claim. Not interest. Not damages. Not compensation for equipment. Nothing.

The only money the tribunal ordered paid: three thousand dollars in costs. Awarded against the Company for a frivolous procedural application they'd filed during the proceedings.

They'd claimed three billion. The tribunal gave them a bill for three thousand.

But it wasn't just the outcome. It was how the tribunal reached it.

The Staged Contract – Complete Vindication

The tribunal adopted our analysis entirely.

They called the contract "STAGED"—used the exact word, in capital letters, as if it were obvious. "Multiple phases contingent on delivery and performance," they wrote.

They accepted our compartmentalisation structure: Category A, Category B, Category C, D, E—the framework I'd discovered in my bathroom and developed in the 187-page post-hearing brief.

They agreed that "the availability of the assets (weapons and ammunition) and other amenities became the benchmark by which milestone payments were made."

Payment wasn't tied to effort. It was tied to delivery.

And they found the Company had failed to deliver.

The Company's Failures – Documented by the Tribunal

The tribunal created a detailed table—forty items, each with dates showing when the shipping process began. Helicopters, vehicles, weapons, ammunition. All from the Company's own documents.

Not one item was delivered within the contracted timeline.

The contract required helicopters within 21 days of payment. The Company's airway bill: January 30, 2015—more than a month late—and that was just the shipping initiation, not the actual arrival.

The contract required vehicles within 14 days—airway bill: February 12, 2015—almost two months late.

And the tribunal noted something remarkable: The Company's contract had stated that helicopters were "in boxes ready to be shipped" when they signed. They'd represented that the equipment was ready. But they didn't ship it for over two months.

The tribunal wrote: "The Claimant could not therefore rely on the absence of regulatory approval as a justification for not supplying at least the helicopters."

The Company's regulatory approval excuse—one of their main defences—was rejected.

Time was Fundamental

The tribunal agreed that time was essential: "The parties clearly intended these timeframes to be essential and crucial to the contract's purpose. The tribunal therefore considers time to be a fundamental term of the contract."

And because time was fundamental, the Company's delays were fatal: "The failure of the Claimant to deliver equipment that was critical to the execution of the war was undoubtedly a breach. The failure to do so, for every day that the equipment ought to have been delivered, constitutes a continuing breach."

Continuing breach. The Company hadn't just failed once—they failed every day the equipment wasn't delivered.

The Staged Contract Analysis – Word for Word

The tribunal concluded exactly what I'd realised in my bathroom that Friday morning in July:

"If the Claimant performs by supplying all the assets in the first category, it should automatically be entitled to payment in the second category. Similarly, if it fails to perform its supply obligation in Category A, it will not be entitled to payment in Category B."

They'd adopted our framework. Used our logic. Agreed with our analysis.

The Company had failed to perform Category A. Therefore, they weren't entitled to payment for Category B, C, D, or E.

The three-billion-dollar claim was mathematically impossible.

The Missing Evidence

The tribunal noted that the Company had withheld critical evidence.

When we'd requested bank statements showing the timing of payments to suppliers, the Company refused to produce them.

The tribunal wrote: "Withholding evidence in law and refusal to bring the evidence is fatal to the Claimant's case."

Fatal. Their own word.

The Company had refused to produce evidence that would have proved or disproved their timeline claims. The tribunal found this fatal to their case.

The Settlement Agreement – Upheld

The Company had claimed duress, coercion, and economic pressure. They said George Sweeny had been forced to sign the End-of-Contract and Closure Agreement.

The tribunal rejected every argument.

No duress: "The facts as stated by all the parties, including Mr Sweeny, do not suggest duress."

No unconscionable bargain: The Company was experienced in military contracts, had drafted both the main contract and the ECCA, and knew the market.

No economic duress: While Sweeny faced financial pressure, "this tension alone was not deemed sufficient to constitute economic duress, especially considering the presence of James Black, who had become known for his role as a mediator."

The settlement was valid. Binding. The Company's claims based on post-settlement events were dismissed in their entirety.

Ashley's Vindication

Colonel Ashley had testified that Nigeria overpaid the Company for the first milestone. His calculations showed the differential.

The tribunal confirmed it: Nigeria had overpaid by US$2,865,769.37—nearly three million dollars more than required.

Ashley had been right. The documentary evidence proved it.

The Complete Victory

I read through all ninety-one pages, taking notes, marking passages.

The tribunal had:

- Adopted our staged contract framework entirely
- Found the Company committed a continuing breach
- Agreed time was fundamental
- Rejected all regulatory approval excuses
- Upheld the settlement agreement
- Confirmed Nigeria overpaid
- Dismissed every one of the Company's claims
- Awarded the Company nothing

We'd saved government three billion dollars.

But there was something else. Something that became clearer with each page I read.

Something missing.

What the Tribunal Never Mentioned

Ninety-one pages. Hundreds of findings on contract interpretation, timeline analysis, witness credibility, payment obligations, breach of contract, and settlement validity.

But on the statements made by the presiding arbitrator during the hearing—"we have our position," "we've formed our impression" before we even presented our defence, the characterisation of the contract as a lease—complete silence.

The Award never mentioned them.

Never explained them.

Never reconciled them with the twenty-five months of deliberation that followed.

The transcript had captured everything. "We have a full picture." "We have our position." Said out loud, in open proceedings, recorded by the court reporter.

I'd challenged the arbitrators based on those kinds of statements and others. Filed a formal challenge under Article 13 of the UNCITRAL Rules. That challenge was part of the official record.

The tribunal had rejected the challenge. That rejection was in the record too.

But in the Award—in the document that would become the authoritative account of these proceedings—the pre-judgment statements simply disappeared.

As if they'd never been said.

The tribunal had been free to address them. To explain what the presiding arbitrator had meant. To reconcile those statements with their claim that they'd carefully considered our defence before ruling.

They chose not to.

Instead, they adopted our staged contract analysis. Agreed with our evidence. Found the Company had failed to perform. Awarded us complete victory.

And in doing so, they made those pre-judgment statements even harder to explain.

If our case was strong enough to warrant complete dismissal of a three-billion-dollar claim—if the law and facts were this clear—what had the presiding arbitrator meant when he announced during the hearing that they already had "a full picture"? That they'd "formed their views"? That they were characterising the contract as a lease before we'd even presented our argument?

The Award didn't answer those questions. It erased them.

The Tribunal's Excuse for the 25-Month Delay

The Award offered what appears to be an explanation for the twenty-five-month deliberation.

"Both Counsel," the tribunal wrote, "failed to respond to subsequent correspondence requesting additional clarification on one or two legal points that the Tribunal encountered in the course of concluding this Award."

One or two legal points. Both counsel—failed to respond.

But the same paragraph admitted: "However, the absence of Counsel's input did not impact this Award in any way."

If our input didn't impact the Award, what took twenty-five months?

And the tribunal didn't stop there. They criticised both sides for delays during the proceedings. They noted the Company had been foreclosed for missing deadlines.

After ruling completely in our favour—after adopting our analysis, agreeing with our evidence, dismissing every claim—the tribunal still made sure to note that we'd been slow to respond to applications. But I submitted all the required processes on time—in fact, in most cases, earlier than required. Never asked for an extension of time. Never delayed for one day.

Twenty-five months after announcing they had "a position." Twenty-five months after post-hearing reply briefs were submitted. Twenty-five months for an Award in what they called a straightforward case.

Of the five years this case lasted, the tribunal allowed the Company eighteen months to submit its pleadings due in forty-five days. Spent twenty-five months writing the Award. But the delays they emphasised in the Award were ours, not theirs. Not the Company's. But ours.

I sat back from the computer screen.

Ninety-one pages. Complete victory. Total vindication of our analysis.

And complete silence on the conduct that had made the past five years so difficult.

The record was perfect. The documentation was complete. Every pre-judgment statement captured, timestamped, preserved.

And it had simply disappeared from the official account.

I forwarded the Award to my team: "Complete victory. Please review and provide comments."

Then I closed my laptop and stared at the ceiling.

We'd won.

We'd saved three billion dollars.

The tribunal had vindicated every argument we'd made.

And they'd erased every concern we'd raised.

That's not a flaw in the system.

That's the system working exactly as designed.

Twenty-Nine Minutes

Then, at 3:16 p.m.—twenty-nine minutes after the first email—came the second message.

I've described my reaction to the disciplinary summons in the opening of this book. What matters now is what it meant.

The charges were clear: imputing bias to the tribunal, attacking the integrity of the arbitrators, bringing the profession into disrepute.

But the only documentary evidence they actually provided was my July 2024 letter expressing concern about the delay in delivering the Award.

No copies of the challenge letters. No copies of the procedural objections. Just that one letter about the delay.

I read it once. Then again.

Then I started laughing.

Because of course they had. Of course.

Of course. Naturally. What else would they do?

The timing was striking: victory and disciplinary charges, twenty-nine minutes apart.

I had challenged the tribunal. I had filed a formal challenge under the UNCITRAL Rules. I had documented concerns about procedural irregularities in multiple letters. I had expressed concern about the delay in issuing the Award.

And I had submitted a post-hearing brief that constrained them to rule in our favour despite what appeared to be their preference.

The disciplinary charges were based on those same letters and challenges.

The Pattern Completes Itself

Twenty-nine minutes.

From complete victory to disciplinary summons: twenty-nine minutes.

The Award was timestamped 2:47 p.m.

The disciplinary charges arrived at 3:16 p.m.

I'd documented the tribunal's conduct for three years. Filed a formal challenge. Written letters expressing concerns. Preserved every procedural irregularity in the record.

And I'd won. Completely. The tribunal adopted my analysis, accepted my evidence, and dismissed the Company's three-billion-dollar claim in its entirety.

But the Award never mentioned the pre-judgment. Never addressed the "we have our position" statements. Never explained the 25-month Delay. Never reconciled anything.

They'd given me victory on the merits while erasing my challenge from the official account.

And now, twenty-nine minutes after delivering that victory, came the consequences for having challenged them at all.

The disciplinary summons mentioned my challenge, but did not include the formal challenge document. My challenge to their independence and impartiality. My documentation of procedural concerns. My expression of worry about the delay in delivering the Award.

All of it—everything I'd carefully preserved in the record—now reframed as professional misconduct. As attacking the tribunal's integrity. As bringing the profession into disrepute.

The system had worked perfectly.

They couldn't deny me victory—the evidence and legal arguments I articulated made that impossible. They couldn't address my challenge—that would require acknowledging it. So they did the only thing they could: they vindicated my case and served me a disciplinary summons for fighting it.

Twenty-nine minutes.

That's how long it took for victory to turn into vulnerability.

The temporal proximity of the Award and the summons was remarkable. But I could not know the arbitrators' motivations with certainty. What I knew was this: I had exercised my professional right and duty to challenge the apparent lack of independence and impartiality, and disciplinary proceedings had followed.

Whether that was a coincidence, a response, or retaliation, others would have to judge.

Twenty-nine minutes between victory and what appeared to be retaliation.

Twenty-nine minutes between vindication and what appeared to be punishment.

It was almost perfectly symmetrical.

I called my team again. "There's something else. I just received a disciplinary summons. Against me. They're claiming professional misconduct based on my letter about the delay."

Silence on the line. Then: "They can't be serious."

"They're serious. It's filed with the Legal Practitioners Disciplinary Committee. Formal charges."

The sequence of events, in my view, gave rise to a reasonable perception of retaliation.

"It appears to be retaliation. I challenged them. I documented their apparent lack of independence and impartiality. I presented evidence that made ruling for the Company very difficult. I constrained them to rule against the party they'd indulged for three years. And now they've filed charges."

"What are you going to do?"

I thought about that. What was I going to do?

"I'm going to defend myself," I said. "I'm going to write my response. I'm going to appear at the hearing. And I'm going to prove that everything I did was in the best interest of my client, within the rules of professional conduct, and in the best traditions of the Bar."

"You sound calm."

"I am calm. Because this doesn't change anything. We won the case. We saved the government three billion dollars. This summons is vengeful, but it's also predictable. They had to do something to save face."

The disciplinary proceedings followed immediately after the Award, giving rise to questions others may draw their own conclusions about.

"Are you going to hire lawyers?"

"No," I said. "I'm going to defend myself. I've been a lawyer for thirty-five years now. I know what I did and why. If they initiated a disciplinary action against me for doing my job, I'll make them explain their reasoning in writing, for the record."

After the call ended, I sat down at my desk with both emails open on my screen.

The Award: complete victory, three billion dollars saved, five years of work vindicated.

The summons: professional charges, disciplinary summons, and retaliation for challenging the tribunal.

I read them both again, side by side. Victory and punishment. Vindication and what appeared to be retaliation.

The paradox was striking. Which raised an uncomfortable question: If the tribunal accepted our evidence and legal arguments—and they had, completely—then what did that say about their conduct during the hearing? About the presiding arbitrator's statement that they already had "a full picture" and "a position" before we'd presented our defence? About his claim they had "formed our impression" before hearing our full case? About his characterisation of the procurement and performance contract as a "lease"? "The equipment was leased, wasn't it?"

If our arguments were correct—correct enough to dismiss three billion dollars in claims—then those statements during the hearing had been either premature judgment or something worse.

The perfect symmetry of a system that rewards evidence but punishes those who challenge institutional conduct. The system had accepted my evidence but seemed unwilling to accept my challenge to its processes. They had ruled in favour of the evidence, but seemed determined to punish the lawyer who had documented what it took to get there.

Through my window, Lagos continued its chaotic dance. Traffic. Commerce. The machinery of a nation that had just avoided losing three billion dollars and didn't even know it yet.

I smiled.

The Wait was over.

Now came the reckoning.

The Other Retaliation

The Award was in our favour. Yes, we had won completely. The three-billion-dollar claim was rejected in its entirety.

But there was something else in the Award that I noticed immediately.

The tribunal's treatment of our costs claim appeared to follow a pattern.

They'd ruled completely in our favour on the merits. Adopted our analysis. Agreed with our evidence. Saved Nigeria three billion dollars.

But when it came to compensating us for five years of work—work that had just achieved total victory—they simply... passed over it.

Under the UNCITRAL Arbitration Rules, the prevailing party is entitled to recover reasonable legal and other costs. I had submitted a detailed claim for US$11,170,000 for my legal costs and expenses. The claim was itemised and quantified: four senior lawyers and two support staff had spent approximately eight thousand hours over five years reading thousands of pages of documents, attending client meetings and discussions, interviewing witnesses, preparing and writing submissions, researching legal principles and authorities, responding to correspondence, and attending virtual and in-person meetings and hearings in a claim of approximately US$3 billion.

Our time chat was there.

The Company did not oppose the claim. They filed no response challenging the amounts. They made no argument that the costs were high or unreasonable. They did not contest the hours worked or the rates charged.

In the normal course of arbitration, when a prevailing party's cost claim is uncontested by the losing party, tribunals grant it in full or make only minimal adjustments.

The tribunal glossed over it entirely.

In their Award, they provided no substantive analysis of the costs. No assessment of reasonableness. No explanation for disallowing an uncontested claim from the prevailing party. They simply moved past it as if it were a minor administrative detail unworthy of consideration.

US$11,170,000. Eight thousand hours. Five years of work. Uncontested by the losing party. And the tribunal said nothing. Denied without explanation.

I thought about the Award's structure.

Ninety-one pages analysing every aspect of the Company's claim. Detailed findings on contract interpretation. Careful analysis of timeline evidence. Thorough discussion of the settlement agreement.

But our costs claim—uncontested, quantified, fully documented, from the prevailing party—dismissed in a few paragraphs with no reasoning.

The same pattern as the pre-judgment statements. What matters to them, they analyse thoroughly. What implicates them, they erase.

The costs Award or lack of it required no explanation because acknowledging why they denied it would require acknowledging what those five years had been like. The procedural battles. The differential treatment. The conduct that made every victory harder than it should have been.

Easier to just deny it. Move on. Provide no reasoning they'd have to defend.

Under the UNCITRAL Rules, costs are within the tribunal's discretion—but that discretion is not absolute. It must be exercised judicially and judiciously. A tribunal cannot simply dismiss or ignore a claim for legal costs without justification. Its decision must be based on the evidence and arguments presented, and it must provide a reasoned explanation for its decision.

If a tribunal decides not to grant costs to a winning party—particularly when those costs are uncontested—it needs to explain its rationale. The discretion exists to ensure fairness, not to enable arbitrary decisions.

The tribunal provided no explanation. No analysis of reasonableness. No finding that the costs were excessive. No reasoning at all.

In my view, this was not the judicial exercise of discretion contemplated by the rules. It appeared to be an arbitrary denial of a legitimate claim by the prevailing party—a claim the losing party hadn't even contested.

I had challenged their apparent lack of independence and impartiality in March 2022. I had documented the pattern of decisions in a formal letter that became part of the permanent record. I had forced them to confront their preferential treatment of the Company. And then I had won the case despite all of it.

The cost denial appeared to follow from the challenge. Not as dramatic as what would come twenty-nine minutes later, but equally deliberate. They couldn't deny us victory on the merits—the evidence made that impossible. But they could punish us financially, and do so in a way that required no explanation, no reasoning, no justification they'd have to defend.

The effect of the unexplained costs decision was to deny recovery despite uncontested evidence.

I made a note of it and moved on to read the rest of the Award. There would be time later to consider what appeared to be an abuse of discretion meant. For now, I needed to understand the full ruling.

But I understood the message. Even in victory, there would be consequences for having challenged them.

The Asymmetric Credibility Pattern

By mid-2022, I'd observed a pattern in how the tribunal engaged with arguments from each side.

When the Company's counsel made a submission—no matter how unsupported by evidence or inconsistent with the contract terms—the tribunal treated it as worthy of serious consideration. They'd ask follow-up questions. They'd explore the implications. They'd give it weight in their procedural rulings.

When we presented arguments backed by documentary evidence and binding legal authority, the tribunal often seemed to discount them before we'd finished speaking.

The Company's witness could make broad, unsubstantiated claims about regulatory delays or equipment delivery, and the tribunal would nod thoughtfully. We could present timestamped shipping manifests proving late delivery, but the tribunal would move on without acknowledging them.

The Company's counsel could argue that the contract was a "lease"—a characterisation nowhere in the contract text—and the presiding arbitrator would adopt that language immediately. We could point to the actual contract provisions showing staged performance obligations, and the tribunal would redirect the discussion.

The pattern wasn't subtle. It was systematic.

This asymmetry shaped my strategic decisions throughout the case. If the tribunal were predisposed to credit the Company's narrative regardless of the evidence, presenting our strongest legal arguments orally during the hearing would accomplish nothing. They'd be dismissed or minimised in the moment, just as our procedural objections had been dismissed for three years.

But a written brief was different. A written brief couldn't be interrupted. It couldn't be redirected. It had to be read in full, considered in its entirety, and, if dismissed, the dismissal had to be explained in the Award—on the permanent record.

This is why I held back the staged contract theory until the post-hearing brief.

Not because the argument wasn't fully developed—I'd had it since July 2022, months before the hearing. Not because it wasn't relevant to the hearing—it was the foundation of our entire defence. But because presenting it orally, in a hearing room where the tribunal had already announced they had "a position," would have allowed them to minimise it, reframe it, or simply ignore it.

In writing, they couldn't do that. They'd have to engage with it seriously or reveal in their Award that they'd dismissed a comprehensive legal argument without adequate consideration.

The tribunal's pattern of treating the Company's unsupported assertions as credible while discounting our documented evidence forced me to adapt my strategy. I couldn't rely on oral advocacy to persuade arbitrators who appeared to have already formed their views. I had to create a written record so thorough, so legally precise, so impossible to dismiss without professional embarrassment, that even a tribunal predisposed against us would have to rule in our favour.

The 187-page post-hearing brief was designed for exactly that purpose. Not to persuade minds already made up, but to constrain the range of professionally defensible outcomes.

It worked. But the fact that such a strategy was necessary—that I had to assume the tribunal would discount sound legal arguments presented orally while crediting unsupported assertions from the opposing party—revealed something troubling about how the proceeding had been conducted.

The Dissent that Changed Nothing

The Award contained an unusual feature: a dissenting opinion authored by the Company-appointed arbitrator. While dissenting opinions are common in court judgments, they are not contemplated by the UNCITRAL Arbitration Rules. In practice, arbitral awards are issued as a single instrument reflecting the majority's view, signed by all arbitrators. A dissent, where it appears, has no operative effect. It does not alter the Award, affect enforcement, or create any independent legal consequence.

The dissenting Award wasn't carefully framed. The dissenting arbitrator expressly accepted the majority's account of the evidence, the factual findings, and the procedural history. He did not dispute the credibility assessments, the documentary record, or the tribunal's reconstruction of events. His disagreement was confined to the legal conclusions drawn from those facts, particularly regarding the validity and effect of the End of Contract and Closure Agreement (settlement agreement).

That framing is significant — and revealing.

A principled dissent ordinarily identifies a legal error: a misstatement of the governing test, the application of an incorrect standard, or a failure to engage with binding authority. This dissent did none of those things. It articulated no alternative legal test for duress or coercion, identified no misapplication of law by the majority, and pointed to no factual finding that could not reasonably support the conclusions reached. Instead, it accepted the facts as found and re-characterised their legal significance, effectively advancing a different evaluative preference rather than demonstrating legal error.

In substance, the dissent disagreed not with the law as applied, but with the outcome itself.

That is not a dissent in arbitration.

That is a losing submission rewritten as judicial prose.

That is advocacy — not adjudication.

That internal contradiction — accepting the evidentiary findings while rejecting the conclusions they compelled — deprived the dissent of jurisprudential force. Without identifying a flaw in the legal framework or its application, the dissent amounted to a restatement of the losing party's position in adjudicative form. It changed nothing. It could change nothing.

Its presence nonetheless served a purpose. Where the majority could neither deny the evidence nor avoid the legal consequences that flowed from it, the dissent provided a symbolic counterweight — an acknowledgement of loss without a legal pathway to reverse it. In that sense, the dissent did not challenge the Award; it merely accompanied it.

Chapter 13

The Silence

Where I describe reactions, motivations, or institutional responses, I do so based on my observations and the record as it appeared to me at the time.

The euphoria lasted about a week.

A week of reading and re-reading the Award. A week of my team celebrating, analysing the tribunal's reasoning, understanding how completely we'd won—a week of calls and messages from colleagues who'd heard the news.

Complete victory. Three-billion-dollar claim dismissed.

But alongside the victory was the reality I'd known was coming: twenty-nine minutes after the Award arrived, so had the preview of what the arbitrators intended to do. What followed created the appearance of retaliation for having challenged the tribunal, documented procedural concerns, and presented evidence that made an adverse ruling increasingly difficult to sustain.

I'd expected it. I'd even predicted it to my team months earlier. But expecting something and experiencing it are different things.

On September 26, 2024—twenty days after receiving original copies of the Award—I sat down to write to my clients. The National Security Adviser and the Attorney General of the Federation. The officials whose offices had engaged me five years earlier to defend Nigeria, against a three-billion-dollar claim, I believed was without merit.

* * * *

The letters were straightforward and professional.

I summarised the outcome: after twenty-five months from the close of the hearing, the tribunal had delivered its decision in our favour, dismissing all of the Claimant's claims against the Federal Government of Nigeria.

I detailed the tribunal's final orders—the dismissal of the claim and the costs awarded in our favour for the Company's breach of confidentiality and for its frivolous applications. I noted our disagreement with the tribunal's refusal to award legal fees, despite our having documented over 8,000 hours of work.

Then I addressed what had happened immediately after our victory:

When the tribunal was taking an excessive amount of time to deliver the Award, we expressed our concern, given the information available to us that the Claimant and its representatives were scheming. As a result of our expression of concern, the arbitrators have initiated disciplinary proceedings against me before the Legal Practitioners Disciplinary Committee (LPDC).

I sent both letters by courier. Then I waited for a response.

* * * *

A week passed. No response.

Two weeks. Nothing.

I called the Director of Civil Litigation at the Ministry of Justice—my direct point of contact throughout the case. The person who had coordinated with me, received my updates, and served as the link between my firm and the government.

The Director didn't answer. I left a message.

The Director never called back.

A few weeks after I sent the letters, I received a brief, careful phone call.

It was the Special Assistant. Or rather, the former Special Assistant—he was no longer in that role. The new administration had brought its own people.

He'd been removed from that position more than a year before the Award arrived. He had no official capacity to help. And even if he wanted to, what could he do?

"Andy, I heard about the Award," he said. "Congratulations. You did what we hoped you would do."

"Thank you. I've written to the NSA and AG—"

"I know. I can't help with that officially. I'm no longer in that office."

There was a long pause.

"But personally," he continued, "I want you to know that what you accomplished mattered. Three billion dollars. Against that tribunal. I know what you faced."

"I'm facing disciplinary proceedings now. Twenty-nine minutes after the Award, the summons arrived."

Another pause. "I heard that too. I'm sorry. That's—" He stopped. "I wish I could do more. But I'm no longer in a position to—"

"I understand."

"For what it's worth, from someone who was there, who saw what you were up against: you did the right thing. You defended Nigeria's interests against difficult odds. That should count for something."

"Should," I agreed.

After we hung up, I sat with that conversation. One person who understood. One person who'd been there. One person who cared.

But no longer in a position to help. He'd been removed from that position more than a year before the Award arrived. He had no official capacity to help. And even if he wanted to, what could he do?

The people who had engaged me—who had sat across from me at that first meeting in June 2019, who had explained the stakes, who had asked me to defend Nigeria's interests—were gone. Transferred. Retired. Moved to other roles. The institutional memory of why this case mattered, of what had been at stake, of the tribunal we'd faced—all of it had left with them. The institution had moved on. New administration. New priorities. New officials who hadn't lived through what we'd fought.

The new officials reviewing my letters in September 2024 had no connection to the case. They hadn't lived through the three years of documented irregularities. They hadn't been there when the Company was getting extension after extension, while we were ordered to work through a pandemic lockdown. They hadn't seen the pattern.

To them, I was just a lawyer who'd won a case—and who now had a disciplinary summons from three Senior Advocates of Nigeria.

One data point they understood. The other required context they didn't have and apparently didn't want.

And I was alone with a three-billion-dollar victory and a disciplinary summons.

I mentioned it to my team during a meeting. "Still nothing from the NSA or AG?"

"Nothing. No acknowledgement. No response. No callback."

One of them said what we were all thinking: "That seems strange for a three-billion-dollar victory."

"New administration," I said. "New officials. No connection to the case. And I have a disciplinary summons."

We moved on to other matters. There was work to be done, other cases to handle, other clients to serve.

But the silence remained.

* * * *

On January 14, 2025—while I was travelling outside Nigeria—the formal summons from the Legal Practitioners Disciplinary Committee was delivered to my office in Lagos by courier.

The charges were as I'd expected: imputing bias to the tribunal, attacking the integrity of arbitrators, bringing the profession into disrepute.

The basis—the gravamen of the charges: my July 2024 letter expressing concern about the twenty-month delay in issuing the Award.

My secretary scanned and emailed the complete summons. I read through it carefully. The Legal Practitioners Disciplinary Committee had the power to suspend or disbar lawyers. These proceedings were serious, formal, quasi-judicial.

But I wasn't angry. I wasn't even particularly worried.

I was ready.

* * * *

My defence took fifteen days of focused work to write.

I structured it methodically:

On challenging the arbitrators for apparent lack of independence and impartiality: I had not just a right but a duty to my client to raise concerns about apparent lack of independence and impartiality. The UNCITRAL Arbitration Rules explicitly provided for such challenges. I had followed the proper procedure, documented specific instances, and acted in accordance with my professional obligations.

On expressing concern about the delay: Twenty months was objectively extraordinary for writing an arbitration Award. My observation was factual. I had not imputed improper motives—I had noted that the delay was unusual and requested expeditious resolution. This was legitimate advocacy, not professional misconduct.

On attacking the profession: I had done nothing of the sort. I had vigorously defended my client, challenged arbitrators whose conduct raised concerns about impartiality, and documented irregularities that needed to be part of the record. Professional conduct requires zealous advocacy within ethical bounds. I had operated well within those bounds throughout.

I included extensive exhibits: transcripts showing the tribunal's favourable treatment of the Company, procedural orders granting extensions without justification, and analyses of the timeline proving the delay was unprecedented.

The response was analytical, precise, and unemotional. Not angry, not defensive. Simply a clear presentation of what had happened and why my conduct had been proper.

Writing it provided an unexpected clarity. For fifteen days, I had the opportunity to lay out—in formal legal argument—everything that had happened in this case. The pattern of decisions I'd observed and documented. The procedural decisions that had consistently favoured the Company. Every instance of differential treatment, supported by the record itself.

I couldn't say all of this at the hearing. Professional courtesy and decorum prevented full candour in the hearing room. But in a formal defence against disciplinary charges, I could be completely honest.

Every concerning decision, documented with citations.

Every procedural irregularity, explained with evidence.

Every example of differential treatment, itemised from the record itself.

It wasn't cathartic in the sense of emotional release. It was cathartic in the sense of intellectual honesty finally expressed openly. The truth, laid out systematically, comprehensively, undeniably.

I submitted the response on February 27, 2025.

* * * *

By summer 2025, I had still not received a response from the government.

Then, in late summer, I learned something that added context to the silence.

Through the same professional channels that had brought me information throughout the case, I heard that the new National Security Adviser was now working with the Company's principal. New projects. New contracts. Business continuing as if the arbitration had never happened.

I shared this information with my team during a meeting.

"You're certain?" one of them asked.

"As certain as I can be without official confirmation. Multiple sources, all consistent."

"So, everything we fought for—"

"Meant we won the case," I interrupted. "It meant the government didn't lose three billion dollars. That matters. The money stayed in Nigeria, available for actual security needs rather than the claims we successfully defended against That's significant."

"But the Company is still operating. Still getting contracts from the very same government it tried to overreach with controversial and highly questionable claims."

"Yes. Different administration, different officials, same patterns. We won a battle. The war continues."

"Would you do it again?"

I didn't hesitate. "Yes. Without question. Because the alternative is becoming complicit, and I won't do that."

* * * *

In early September 2025—exactly one year after the first letter to the NSA and AG—I wrote a second letter to the National Security Adviser.

This one was more direct. I reminded him of the case, the victory, and my previous letter dated September 26, 2024. I noted that I had received no acknowledgement.

I explained the disciplinary proceedings:

I vigorously defended the Federal Government and the national interest before a hostile tribunal in the best traditions of the Bar. The result was a complete victory against all odds that saved the nation about US$3 billion. I am now facing disciplinary proceedings initiated by the very arbitrators I formally challenged for apparent abuse and misuse of arbitral authority throughout the proceedings.

I made a modest request:

I respectfully request that your office: (a) Acknowledge receipt of the original copy of the arbitral Award; (b) Recognise the significance of this victory for the Federal Government and the nation; (c) Provide such support as may be appropriate in relation to the disciplinary proceedings I now face.

I concluded: *I served the Federal Government faithfully and at considerable personal cost. The result speaks for itself. I believe the circumstances warrant the government's acknowledgement and support.*

I sent it by courier. The courier confirmed delivery.

No response came.

* * * *

The disciplinary hearing is yet to be scheduled.

I would appear personally. I would present my defence. If the arbitrators testified, I would cross-examine them. I would demonstrate that my conduct had been proper, professional, and in my client's best interest throughout.

"You sound confident."

"I am confident. Because I know what I did and why. I defended my client zealously. I challenged arbitrators whose conduct raised serious concerns about impartiality. I documented concerning conduct that needed to be part of the record."

"Would you still take the case?"

"Absolutely. Without hesitation. Because it was the right thing to do, but I would be realistic about expectations from the start. I would know from the beginning that winning wouldn't guarantee gratitude."

* * * *

By December 2025, I had accepted the silence as final.

The government had received my letters—both of them. They had read the Award. They understood we'd won. They knew I was facing disciplinary proceedings that followed my defence of their interests.

And they had chosen not to respond.

That choice told me everything I needed to know about institutional loyalty in a system where challenging institutional irregularities is more dangerous than accepting it quietly.

The tribunal's hostility had been honest and direct. Their conduct had been consistent throughout. Their response was consistent with the pattern I had documented.

The government's silence was different. Passive rather than active. But just as revealing about how institutions operate when principles conflict with convenience.

The disciplinary hearing would come. I would defend myself. I would demonstrate that my conduct was proper. And I would do it with the same professional thoroughness that had carried me through five years of the arbitration.

Not because institutions supported that approach. But it was the only approach consistent with the principles that had led me to take this case in the first place.

Outside my window, Lagos continued its rhythm. Traffic. Commerce. Government offices are conducting business as usual.

I'd saved three billion dollars. I'd documented serious procedural concerns. I'd proven that evidence and law could still prevail against a difficult procedural environment.

The government's silence didn't change any of that. It simply revealed which principles they valued and which they didn't.

And that, in the end, was information worth having.

Epilogue

The observations and conclusions in this Epilogue reflect my professional experience and assessment of events as they appeared to me at the time, based on the record and circumstances then known.

Five years. Three billion dollars. A tribunal whose conduct raised serious concerns. Complete victory. Disciplinary summons that followed immediately thereafter. Government silence.

Looking back at this experience from where I stand now—awaiting a disciplinary hearing, having received no acknowledgement from the government I defended—I find myself reflecting not on whether I'd do it again, but on what this case reveals about the systems we operate within.

I would take the case again. Without hesitation. Because it was the right thing to do.

But I wouldn't approach it the same way. I wouldn't put in 8,000 hours for a client that views such effort as routine rather than exceptional. I wouldn't sacrifice as much for institutions that value compliance over courage.

The question isn't whether to challenge inappropriate conduct. That answer remains constant: yes, always. The question is understanding clearly what that challenge costs and who bears that cost.

The Vulnerability of Ad Hoc Arbitration

This case exposed significant vulnerabilities in ad hoc arbitration as currently practised, particularly in jurisdictions with weak institutional safeguards.

Ad hoc arbitration under the UNCITRAL Rules does provide recourse mechanisms. Article 13 allows parties to challenge arbitrators for lack of independence or impartiality. Article 14 permits the removal of arbitrators who fail to act. National courts can review jurisdictional decisions and set aside Awards for serious procedural irregularities.

But these mechanisms proved inadequate in this case.

When I challenged the arbitrators under Article 13, the challenge was decided by the very tribunal I was challenging—the presiding arbitrator and his co-arbitrators ruled on their own impartiality.

I attempted to invoke the appointing authority—the mechanism designed to provide independent review of arbitrator challenges. Under the UNCITRAL Rules, this process can proceed without the other party's cooperation. But it takes time—potentially months. It requires resources and legal fees. And crucially, the arbitration doesn't pause while the challenge is pending. Deadlines continue. Hearings get scheduled. The case advances.

In institutional arbitration, challenges are handled by dedicated administrative staff with established procedures and timelines. The institution can suspend proceedings pending resolution. The machinery exists to handle these issues efficiently without derailing the substantive case.

In ad hoc arbitration, you're pursuing the appointing authority process while simultaneously preparing for hearings, meeting filing deadlines, and defending a three-billion-dollar claim. The mechanism exists in theory, but the practical burden of using it while maintaining a robust defence can be prohibitive.

This is the real choice the ad hoc arbitration forces: pursue every available procedural remedy despite the time and cost burden, or focus your finite resources on building a substantive case so compelling that procedural concerns become secondary—so strong that the tribunal would have no choice but to rule in our favour despite any concerning patterns.

I chose the latter. I believed—correctly, as it turned out—that evidence and legal arguments could be made so compelling that even a tribunal exhibiting concerning conduct would be constrained to rule properly.

But that choice shouldn't have been necessary.

The UNCITRAL Rules are premised on an assumption of good faith. They presuppose that arbitrators will exercise discretion impartially, that they are conversant with arbitral process and jurisprudence, and that challenges will be addressed promptly—without distorting or derailing the substantive proceedings.

This case demonstrated what happens when those assumptions prove unfounded—when the tribunal advances proceedings despite unresolved impartiality concerns, and when the only practical recourse becomes building a case so unassailable that concerning conduct becomes irrelevant.

In institutional arbitration—conducted under the ICC, LCIA, or similar bodies—there are additional layers of oversight. Institutions can replace arbitrators. They review procedural orders. They scrutinise costs and timelines. They maintain standards that supplement the rules themselves. No arbitral institution would allow a party to file pleadings required within forty-five days, eighteen months later, without serious justification. No arbitral institution would allow an arbitral tribunal twenty-five months to write an Award, as in this case.

In ad hoc arbitration, particularly in jurisdictions where judicial oversight is slow or uncertain, these additional safeguards don't exist.

When arbitrators grant endless extensions to one party while denying them to another, when they accept incomplete submissions or waive mandatory requirements of the rule for the benefit of a party, and when they make statements suggesting they've formed views before hearing the full case, the recourse mechanisms provided by the UNCITRAL Rules may prove theoretical rather than practical.

You can challenge under Article 13—but if the challenged arbitrators decide their own challenge, and pursuing the appointing authority review means months of delay while the case advances, what is the practical remedy?

You can seek court intervention—but judicial review comes only after years have passed and procedural damage has been done.

You can build a record for setting aside the Award, but that provides no protection during the proceedings themselves.

This case demonstrates that ad hoc arbitration in jurisdictions with weak oversight can create opportunities for concerning conduct that institutional arbitration's additional safeguards and enforcement mechanisms might prevent or quickly correct.

These structural vulnerabilities were compounded by delays that undermined arbitration's fundamental purpose.

This case took five years. Of that, the Company spent eighteen months submitting pleadings that should have been filed within forty-five days under the Rules. The tribunal spent twenty-five months writing the Award after the hearing closed.

These delays defeated the intent, spirit, and essence of arbitration itself.

Arbitration exists as an alternative to litigation precisely because it promises efficiency. Parties choose arbitration to avoid the glacial pace of courts. They pay arbitrators' fees specifically to secure faster resolution. When arbitration becomes as slow as—or slower than—the courts it's meant to replace, it loses its fundamental justification.

The eighteen-month extension granted to the Company—without any requirement that they request it before deadlines passed, without serious justification, without consequence—established a precedent that undermines arbitral discipline. This is the practice that has nearly destroyed Nigeria's judicial system: deadlines ignored, extensions granted reflexively, proceedings dragging on indefinitely while parties suffer.

That practice is now creeping into arbitration.

But the tribunal's twenty-five-month delay in delivering the Award was even more troubling. As I wrote in one of my submissions, twenty-five months is an unreasonable amount of time to write an Award, especially when the tribunal gave the parties only thirty days to submit post-hearing briefs. If parties can research, analyse, and write comprehensive legal arguments in thirty days, experienced arbitrators should not require twenty-five months to evaluate those arguments and reach a decision.

* * * *

The tribunal offered an explanation in the Award itself. Both counsel, they claimed, had "failed to respond to subsequent correspondence requesting additional clarification on one or two legal points that the tribunal encountered in the course of concluding this Award."

One or two legal points that required clarification.

But the same paragraph admitted something remarkable: "However, the absence of Counsel's input did not impact this Award in any way."

Read that again. The tribunal claimed our failure to respond to clarification requests delayed the Award. Then it admitted that our response wouldn't have changed anything.

If our response "wouldn't have changed anything," why request the clarification?

If our input didn't impact the Award, what took twenty-five months?

The tribunal also criticised both sides for delays during the proceedings.

But here are the facts: I submitted all required documents on time. I never asked for an extension. I never delayed proceedings by a single day. The Company, by contrast, took eighteen months to file pleadings due in forty-five days and missed multiple deadlines. And the tribunal accommodated these without question.

Yet in the Award, after ruling completely in our favour—after adopting our analysis, agreeing with our evidence, dismissing every claim—the tribunal made sure to note that we'd been slow to respond to applications.

Of the five years of the arbitration, the tribunal allowed the Company eighteen months for pleadings that should have taken forty-five days. They spent twenty-five months writing the Award. But the delays they emphasised in the Award were ours, not theirs.

This pattern of deflection—criticising others for delays while engaging in far worse delays themselves—reveals something important about institutional accountability. Or rather, the lack of it.

For an arbitral tribunal composed of three highly experienced senior lawyers, each with decades of practice, to conduct a case for three years—and then require more than two additional years to produce an Award—says even more about the state of arbitral practice in this jurisdiction. The complexity was not in the case. The facts were straightforward. The evidence was clear. The law was settled. The delay was a choice. Whether that choice reflected indecision, institutional dysfunction, or something much worse, I cannot say with certainty. But twenty-five months to produce an Award in a case of this clarity is not a reflection of diligence; it is a symptom of a system that has lost its way—it is evidence of a system unwilling to confront the consequences of its own process.

* * * *

To put this in context: the median duration of international arbitration from case initiation to final Award is between ten and sixteen months. Post-hearing, a typical arbitral Award is issued within three to six months of final submissions. Complex cases—multi-party disputes, construction arbitrations, intellectual property matters—might take longer, perhaps six to twelve months post-hearing.

But there was nothing procedurally complicated about this arbitration. The contract was straightforward: procurement and performance over defined stages. The issues were clear: Did the Company deliver what they claimed? Was the settlement agreement valid? Were they entitled to three billion dollars for equipment never provided? The tribunal simply needed to evaluate the evidence, apply well-established contract law principles, and write its decision.

Twenty-five months exceeded the entire typical duration of many international arbitrations from filing to Award. It was more than four times the standard post-hearing timeframe. For a case with clear issues and comprehensive briefs, such a delay cannot be explained by complexity or workload. It raises questions about what was happening during those twenty-five months. Especially when the tribunal had announced during the hearing that they already had "a position."

Justice delayed is justice denied. This principle applies as much to arbitration as to litigation.

Inordinate delay in rendering an arbitral Award undermines the raison d'être of arbitration. It weakens public confidence in the arbitral process. It denies justice to the winning party during the delay—in this case, leaving Nigeria exposed to a three-billion-dollar claim for more than two years after we'd proven it should be dismissed. Unreasonable delays negatively affect the quality of the Award and create opportunities for external pressures to influence outcomes.

The solution is straightforward: time limits for arbitral Awards, just as Nigeria's Constitution provides for delivering judgments in court. The UNCITRAL Rules should establish maximum timeframes. Institutional arbitration already does this—many institutions require Awards within specific periods after hearings close, with extensions requiring justification.

Ad hoc arbitration needs similar discipline. Without it, delays will continue to undermine the process, and parties will lose faith in arbitration as a viable alternative to litigation.

This case demonstrated both problems: procedural latitude that allowed endless extensions to one party, and deliberative delay that kept the outcome uncertain long after the evidence and law had made it clear. Both must be addressed if arbitration is to serve its intended purpose.

The UNCITRAL Rules provide a framework. But a framework is only as strong as the commitment of those who operate within it—and the practical effectiveness of its mechanisms when challenged.

Seniority Does Not Equal Competence

One of the most troubling aspects of this case was the arbitrators' credentials. All three were Senior Advocates of Nigeria—a designation reserved for distinguished lawyers of achievement.

But being a senior or "titled lawyer" does not necessarily make one a good arbitrator—the cowl does not make the monk.

Importantly, the skills required for advocacy are different from those needed for adjudication. A highly regarded advocate may be comfortable with partisanship and with aggressively advancing one side's interests in pursuit of results in the courtroom. An arbitrator must be neutral, analytical, and committed to procedural discipline and fairness above outcome preference.

Throughout this arbitration, I observed Senior Advocates—lawyers with decades of experience, reputations built on complex litigation, and standing earned through professional achievement—make procedural choices and decisions that I believed raised serious questions about fairness and the appearance of independence and impartiality.

Their seniority didn't guarantee impartiality. If anything, it may have insulated them from accountability. Their reputations created a presumption of fairness that made challenging them more difficult. Their status as Senior Advocates made others reluctant to publicly question their conduct.

The assumption that experience automatically translates to competence and fairness is dangerous. Some of the most experienced may face less scrutiny of their decisions, precisely because their reputations can shield conduct that might be questioned more readily in less established practitioners.

The arbitration community—in Nigeria and internationally—needs to recognise this. Selection of arbitrators should evaluate not only credentials and experience but also deep knowledge of arbitral process, temperament, demonstrated neutrality, and commitment to procedural fairness. References should come from lawyers who've appeared before them, not just colleagues who've worked alongside them.

Seniority should be considered. But it should never be sufficient on its own.

When Documentation Disappears

This case also exposed a subtler vulnerability—one less visible than delay or procedural indulgence, but more troubling in its implications: the limits of documentation in systems where those being challenged also control the official account.

The UNCITRAL Rules provide mechanisms for raising concerns about arbitral conduct. Article 13 allows parties to challenge arbitrators for lack of independence or impartiality. Hearings are transcribed. Procedural steps are recorded. In theory, the record preserves what occurred.

I relied on those mechanisms.

The Disappearing Challenge

Before the hearing, I formally challenged the presiding arbitrator and the Claimant-appointed arbitrator under Article 13, based on specific statements and a documented pattern of procedural conduct that, in my professional assessment, gave rise to justifiable doubts as to independence and impartiality. The challenge was detailed, evidenced, and properly filed.

The tribunal rejected the challenge. That was their right under the Rules.

What followed, however, was revealing.

The —ninety-one pages analysing contract interpretation, evidentiary standards, witness credibility, and legal principles—made no reference to the challenge at all. Not its existence. Not its grounds. Not the tribunal's reasoning in rejecting it. The procedural history presented in the Award simply omitted that this challenge had ever occurred.

A formal application questioning the tribunal's independence had been made, ruled upon, and documented. Yet in the Award—the document that becomes the authoritative account for purposes of review and enforcement—it effectively did not exist.

The Disappearing Pre-Judgment

A separate, equally troubling omission concerned what occurred during the hearing itself.

During the proceedings, the presiding arbitrator made statements indicating that the tribunal had already formed views on key issues before hearing the Respondent's defence. At one point, he stated: "We have a full picture of what may have happened... we have our position as we listen." This was said before the Respondent's witnesses testified, before its evidence was presented, and before its legal arguments were made.

On other occasions, the presiding arbitrator characterised the contract as a lease, adopting the Company's framing of the agreement before the Respondent had presented its contractual analysis or addressed that characterisation.

These statements were not casual remarks. They went to the heart of adjudicative neutrality. They were captured verbatim in the transcript. They were preserved as part of the official record. They were expressly raised again in my post-hearing submissions.

The Award made no mention of them.

There was no attempt to explain what was meant, to reconcile those statements with the tribunal's assertion that it had approached the defence with an open mind, or to address why such remarks did not affect the appearance of impartiality. The transcript showed one thing. The Award said nothing. And the gap between them simply disappeared.

The Structural Vulnerability

These two omissions—the pre-hearing challenge and the hearing-stage pre-judgment—reveal the same structural problem.

When the only body empowered to assess arbitrator conduct is the tribunal itself, accountability depends entirely on self-review. Arbitrators may rule on challenges to their own impartiality and then issue Awards that omit any reference to the conduct being challenged. Statements preserved in the transcript may simply vanish from the narrative that ultimately matters.

This is the most insidious vulnerability of all: when the only people who can review arbitrator conduct are the arbitrators themselves, the record becomes whatever they say it is.

In court proceedings, judges address recusal applications in reasoned decisions. Appellate courts review those determinations. Legal standards govern when impartiality concerns require intervention. The system, however imperfect, contains checks.

In ad hoc arbitration—particularly in jurisdictions with limited or deferential judicial oversight—those checks are often absent. The Award becomes the beginning and end of accountability. What it omits is rarely examined.

This creates a troubling dynamic. A party may challenge properly, document meticulously, preserve the transcript, and raise concerns again in post-hearing submissions—yet still watch those issues disappear into an Award that tells a different story through silence rather than contradiction.

That is not a failure of diligence. It is a limitation of the system itself.

When documentation exists but accountability depends on those being documented, the record becomes whatever is acknowledged. Everything else, however carefully preserved, fades from view.

The Paradox of Complete Vindication

The tribunal's complete adoption of our case created an uncomfortable paradox.

If our arguments were correct—correct enough to dismiss three billion dollars in claims—then what do the pre-judgment statements mean?

Consider the logic.

During the hearing, the tribunal stated that it had "a full picture" and had "formed a position" after hearing only the Company's case. This was before our defence. Before our evidence. Before our legal arguments.

What followed was twenty-five months of deliberation.

When the Award finally arrived, it adopted our case in its entirety. The tribunal accepted our entire staged contract framework. Used the exact terminology we'd developed. Agreed the contract was "STAGED"—multiple phases contingent on delivery. Found the Company had failed Category A, making payment for Categories B, C, D, and E impossible. Confirmed the Company committed "continuing breach." Upheld the settlement agreement. Rejected every defence the Company offered.

Complete vindication.

This produces an unavoidable tension.

If the case was sufficiently complex to require twenty-five months of deliberation, how could any "position" have been formed before the defence was heard?

And if the case was sufficiently straightforward to justify dismissal of a three-billion-dollar claim in full, why did it require twenty-five months to reach that conclusion?

Both propositions cannot be true at the same time. Yet in a system without meaningful oversight, neither proposition needs to be explained.

Complete vindication on the merits had an ironic effect. It rendered the procedural concerns simultaneously more troubling and less actionable. Had the tribunal ruled against us, the procedural record would have been central to any challenge of the Award. But because the evidence compelled a result in our favour, those concerns were left without a forum for resolution.

The tribunal vindicated our case while erasing its own conduct. It gave us victory on the merits while removing any basis to question how it had approached them. By adopting our framework so completely, it ensured that the appearance of pre-judgment became legally irrelevant.

They could not deny us victory—the evidence and legal analysis made that impossible. They could not defend the pre-judgment—the transcript preserved it too clearly. So they did the only thing left to them: they ruled in our favour and omitted the pre-judgment entirely from the authoritative account.

The transcript exists. The challenge exists. The record exists.

But the Award—the document that governs review, enforcement, and historical memory—says none of it happened.

This is how systems protect themselves: not by defending their conduct, but by erasing it from the official narrative.

Twenty-nine minutes after delivering that Award, I received disciplinary charges for having challenged them.

Vindication and punishment. Victory and retaliation.

All within half an hour.

The Professional Challenge

In substantive terms, this was the easiest case I have handled in thirty-five years of legal practice and yet the most challenging.

It was easy because the facts were clear, the evidence was overwhelming, and the law was settled. There was no genuine legal controversy. No factual ambiguity. No evidentiary gap. The Company's claims were fiction—trumped up. Our defence was documented reality.

But it was challenging in a way no case should be: I had to find a way to articulate the facts, marshal the evidence, and present the law in a manner that would make it impossible for a tribunal that had appeared to pre-judge the case on the record to avoid reaching the correct decision. I wasn't writing to persuade. I was writing to create a record so clear, so comprehensive, and so unassailable that even a tribunal determined to rule against us would struggle to justify doing so.

That is not advocacy in the traditional sense. That is defensive documentation. Writing not to convince, but to constrain. Marshalling evidence not to illuminate, but to make denial impossible.

And the fact that such an approach was necessary—that I had to assume the tribunal had already decided and work backwards from that assumption—reveals everything wrong with what this process had become.

When You Fight Corruption

Nigeria's experience, as I wrote in my letters to the government, is that when you fight corruption, corruption viciously fights back.

In my experience, this case illustrated that principle with unusual clarity.

I challenged arbitrators whose conduct raised serious concerns about impartiality. I documented their pattern of decisions with specific examples and citations to the record. I filed formal challenges under the UNCITRAL Rules. I refused to accept concerning procedural decisions quietly.

The result: An Award dismissing the controversial and highly questionable claim entirely. Complete vindication on the merits, followed within twenty-nine minutes by disciplinary Summons for having raised the concerns that made such vigorous defence necessary.

The temporal proximity—less than half an hour between the Award and the summons—gave rise to questions that others may assess as they see fit. What I know with certainty is that I had exercised my right under the UNCITRAL Arbitration Rules to challenge conduct I believed compromised procedural fairness, and that disciplinary proceedings followed.

The government, which I saved three billion dollars, responded with silence. The institutions I'd hoped would recognise integrity as valuable instead treated it as inconvenient.

This is the reality of challenging impropriety in compromised systems. The system protects itself. It punishes those who expose its failures. It rewards compliance and penalises resistance.

I knew this intellectually before taking this case. I understand it viscerally now.

But that knowledge doesn't change the fundamental choice. Accept problematic conduct quietly, or challenge it and bear the consequences. There is no third option where you challenge impropriety and emerge unscathed.

The question becomes: what kind of professional do you want to be? What principles are you willing to sacrifice for institutional acceptance?

For me, those answers remain clear. I will always challenge abuse of power. I will always document impropriety when I encounter it. I will always zealously defend my clients' interests, even when that defence makes me unpopular with those wielding compromised authority.

But I now understand, more clearly than ever, that institutions don't reward such principles. They tolerate them when convenient and punish them when costly.

Why They Did It

For the Claimant and its counsel to initiate—and pursue for five years, first in court and then in arbitration—a claim devoid of factual, evidential, or legal merit is revealing of something fundamental about what has gone wrong with our justice system. It reflects a systemic dysfunction in which litigation and arbitration are treated not as processes governed by law and evidence, but as methodical gambles premised on the search for a forum where rules of law and basic common sense might be disregarded. The objective was not justice, but the identification of a forum willing to dispense with it.

What Changed

This experience hasn't changed how I practice law. I still take cases based on principle rather than convenience. I still challenge abuse of authority when I encounter it. I still believe evidence and law should determine outcomes.

But it has completely changed how I see and relate to my country's institutions.

What this case ultimately revealed to me, with unsettling clarity, is that Nigeria is an orphan.

It is a country that many who encounter it seek to take advantage of, yet few feel any obligation to protect. Not its leaders. Not its officials. Not even, at times, its own citizens. The systems entrusted with defending its interests are too often repurposed to exploit its vulnerabilities. And so it moves through the world exposed—rich in promise, but unshielded by those entrusted with its care.

Before this case, I understood these realities in the abstract. I knew corruption existed. I knew institutional bias was possible. I knew relationships and influence could, in some circumstances, outweigh legal merit.

But I had believed—perhaps naively—that outcomes still mattered. That saving three billion dollars would earn acknowledgement, if not gratitude. That doing the job properly would carry institutional value, even if the process had been difficult.

The year of silence following our victory taught me otherwise.

Institutions value compliance, not courage. They reward those who don't make trouble, not those who raise difficult questions or document concerning conduct. They protect themselves and their comfortable relationships, not the principles they claim to uphold.

The government I defended has continued working with the Company's principal—the same person who brought a controversial and highly questionable three-billion-dollar claim we successfully defended against: new administration, new contracts, business as usual. As if nothing had happened.

Meanwhile, I face disciplinary proceedings for having defended that same government too vigorously, too honestly, with too much documentation of the concerning conduct I observed.

The lesson is clear: institutions prefer lawyers who don't challenge impropriety. They don't want warriors against improper conduct. They want lawyers who navigate it quietly, who don't document it for the permanent record.

I can't be that kind of lawyer. But I now understand the cost of refusing.

A Message for Nigeria

Ad hoc arbitration, as currently structured and practised in Nigeria, is deeply vulnerable to abuse. This case proved that conclusively.

Without institutional oversight, without simplified mechanisms for replacing arbitrators when concerns arise, and without standards enforced by supervising authorities, the system invites exactly the kind of problems this case exposed.

The solution isn't to abandon arbitration. International commerce requires dispute resolution mechanisms that are faster and more flexible than traditional litigation.

But Nigeria needs to adopt and strengthen institutional arbitration frameworks. Encourage parties to use established arbitral institutions with oversight mechanisms. Develop local institutions with international standards. Create judicial systems capable of meaningfully reviewing arbitral misconduct.

Most importantly, recognise that seniority and reputation do not guarantee integrity and competence. That Senior lawyers can be prejudiced and partial. That distinguished lawyers may struggle with the transition from advocacy to adjudication. That credentials are not substitutes for accountability.

The three billion dollars saved in this case could easily have been lost with a different outcome. The only thing that prevented that loss was evidence so overwhelming and legal arguments so compelling that even a tribunal that appeared, on the record, to have formed its views in advance and pre-judged the contract as a lease couldn't escape their force.

But Nigeria cannot build a system that relies on lawyers constructing unanswerable cases. Cases cannot be won only when the evidence and arguments rise to a standard that leaves no room for interpretation. If our case had been merely strong rather than overwhelming, if our arguments had been persuasive rather than dispositive, if we had constructed our defence based on a higher balance of probabilities only, the outcome might have been different despite the merits.

That's not the standard. A functioning system must produce correct outcomes based on the preponderance of evidence and sound legal reasoning—not only when a case is so one-sided that even a compromised process cannot justify ruling otherwise.

That's not accountability. That's hoping the facts are strong enough to overcome institutional failures.

Nigeria deserves better than hope.

That shouldn't be the standard. That shouldn't be necessary.

Nigeria's institutions—legal, governmental, and professional—need to decide whether they value integrity or merely the appearance of it. Whether they'll protect those who challenge impropriety or abandon them to retaliation. Whether principles matter or only power.

This case provided an answer to those questions. Not the answer I'd hoped for, but a clear one nonetheless.

Looking Forward

The disciplinary hearing will come. I'll present my defence. I'll demonstrate that my conduct was proper, professional, and in accordance with my obligations to my client and in the best traditions of the Bar.

I'm confident about the outcome because I know what I did and why. The challenge I filed was warranted. Every objection I raised was supported by the record. Every concern I expressed was legitimate.

But regardless of that outcome, I know this: I defended Nigeria's interests when others wouldn't or couldn't. I challenged impropriety and problematic conduct when it would have been easier to accept it. I documented concerning patterns, knowing it would make me a target.

I also learned the limits of documentation in systems that rely on self-review. I challenged properly, preserved the record, and raised concerns at every stage available to me. Yet material events—both the challenge itself and statements made during the hearing—simply vanished from the Award that became the official account. That experience clarified a hard truth: when those whose conduct is questioned also control the narrative, the record becomes whatever is acknowledged, and everything else fades from view.

And I'd do it again.

Not because institutions value such choices. But because integrity requires them.

The case is over. The victory is secured. The three billion dollars remained in Nigeria, available for legitimate security needs rather than being siphoned off through highly controversial, deeply flawed, and questionable claims.

That matters.

The government's silence, the tribunal's retaliation, the institutional indifference—those matter too, but differently. They reveal systems that need changing, principles that need defending, and a profession that needs more lawyers willing to pay the cost of integrity.

Five years of my life went into this case. Eight thousand hours of work. A disciplinary summons. A year of silence from the government I defended.

Was it worth it?

Ask me that question when I'm facing a different choice— accept improper conduct quietly or challenge it and bear the consequences—and you'll have your answer.

Some fights are worth having regardless of the cost.

This was one of them.

www.ingramcontent.com/pod-product-compliance
Lightning Source LLC
Chambersburg PA
CBHW031321230926
51848CB00001B/47
9789786845708